PEACE: THE CONTROL OF NATIONAL POWER

A GUIDE FOR THE CONCERNED CITIZEN
ON PROBLEMS OF DISARMAMENT AND
STRENGTHENING OF THE UNITED NATIONS

PEACE: THE CONTROL OF NATIONAL POWER

by PHILIP VAN SLYCK

With a preface by Senator Hubert H. Humphrey

BEACON PRESS • BOSTON

To CHARLES A. HOGAN
and his colleagues of the UN Secretariat —
builders of an international civil service.

Errata —
The second paragraph on page xv should read:

As a service to seminars and discussion groups, additional copies of this book may be ordered direct from the Fund for Education at $1.25 each for five or more copies.

A NOTE ABOUT THIS BOOK

A PRELIMINARY EDITION OF THIS BOOK WAS PUBLISHED in March 1963 and was tested in the spring of 1963 by fifteen institutions and groups, including the World Peace Through Law Committee of the Colorado State Bar Association, the local chapters of several voluntary organizations, a combined faculty-student group at Choate School, by the University of South Dakota and St. Xavier College in undergraduate courses and by two adult seminars at the University of Syracuse. It was also submitted for critical appraisal to a number of leaders of voluntary organizations and to scholars in various fields. This first edition reflects the experience of the test program as well as many of the suggestions from scholars and organization leaders.

In view of this effort, it is hoped that this *Guide* will be useful to university and cooperative extension services, voluntary organizations and groups interested in foreign affairs, and to student groups and concerned citizens who wish to form their own seminars.

The author wishes to express his appreciation to a number of friends and colleagues who were generous to review and comment on various drafts of this manuscript. Special thanks are due the following for their extensive and constructive suggestions: the Hon. Harlan Cleveland, Miss Nancy L. Hoepli, Charles A. Hogan, Grant S. McClellan, Miss Tanya Melich and Saul Mendlovitz.

PREFACE

IN NO AREA OF PUBLIC POLICY HAVE THE BASIC presuppositions of most of us proved more irrelevant to the times than on the subject of war and peace. Despite the almost universal expression of the desire for peace (with Communist China conspicuous for its isolated dissent); despite, too, the widespread verbal recognition of the horrors of thermonuclear war, the fact remains that foreign policy today is often discussed as if war were still the extension of diplomacy.

Such blindness is frightening. It has already led to Khrushchev's desperate gamble in Cuba—a gamble impossible to reconcile with his numerous on-the-record statements about there being no winner in any nuclear contest. It is evident right now in the quest for "independence" in foreign policy through the development of small stocks of nuclear weapons. It likewise underlies the illusory belief that in multiplication and diversification of such weapons there is safety.

Fortunately, none of these mistaken assumptions have been put to the ultimate test. Meanwhile, however, we have had to watch the massive diversion of resources from a thousand and one constructive purposes to the accumulation of weapons we dare not use. Over 100 billion dollars are now being spent annually by the nations of the world on armaments. To think what human suffering could have been alleviated by these sums, what new opportunities realized, is heartbreaking.

Napoleon once said that war was too important a matter to be left to generals. I would say that war—and peace—are questions too basic to be left only to politicians. No citizen can afford to be indifferent to the effect of preparations for a possible nuclear war on the potentialities for domestic welfare and constructive aid abroad. No member of a democracy can rightfully refrain from taking his part in the debate over policies of literally life-and-death importance not only to himself but to all men.

Politicians in a free society are on the whole as hardworking and as well-meaning as any members of the community. How well they discharge their responsibilities, however, depends very largely on how well they can communicate with those from whom they must draw their support. There is nothing simple about a foreign policy appropriate to the rapidly changing and increasingly dangerous world in which we live. To explain this policy successfully, one must have a sophisticated and discriminating audience. Where such an audience is lacking, communication fails. And when this happens too often, the temptation—indeed, the necessity—to simplify recklessly becomes irresistible.

It is only half true, then, to say that in a democracy the politicians must listen to the people in matters of life and death. They must listen —but the people must also have something to say. Participation is the responsibility of every citizen; but the participation must be responsible.

An indispensable prerequisite for responsible participation in public affairs is sustained study and discussion. Independent reading is valuable, but I know from my own experience that there is no substitute for the testing of one's views through the give-and-take of discussion. This, it seems to me, is the unique value of Mr. Van Slyck's guide to the problems of disarmament and strengthening of the United Nations. Specifically designed for use by voluntary discussion groups, it identifies and develops its central themes in such a way as to ensure fruitful discussion of these vitally important topics.

To overcome the intellectual lag in popular attitudes toward war and peace is the major challenge facing every nation today. It seems to me that Mr. Van Slyck's volume is a notable effort to meet this challenge.

HUBERT H. HUMPHREY,
United States Senate

TABLE OF CONTENTS

TABLE OF CONTENTS

TABLE OF CONTENTS

TABLE OF CONTENTS

INTRODUCTION

VIRTUALLY EVERY AMERICAN HAS SOME FAMILIARITY with the issues discussed in this book, since these are issues drawn from headline events of recent history: the Soviet missile challenge in Cuba, the controversial United Nations peace-keeping effort in the Congo, the perennial stalemate in disarmament negotiations, the recent treaty for a limited test ban, the threatened bankruptcy of the UN, current deadlocks in big-power diplomacy and other recurring symptoms of world disorder.

These events, however, are only the raw materials of this book. The purpose of the following pages is to help the concerned citizen see, in meaningful perspective, the large events and dominant trends of these fast-moving times. The persistent question before the reader is, How does the present world system operate; how is it changing; can it be made to operate in a more stable and less war-prone way?

This book does not argue for a particular policy or program. It does serve as a guide, however, to the principal theories and proposals now under discussion. The thoughtful reader will make up his own mind, but he may find the task more manageable with the aid of this guide.

Each of the nine essays in this book analyzes some important aspect of the present world system — from the use of force to the uses of law. Each essay also discusses various proposals for modifying, strengthening or restructuring the present world system, including proposals for strengthened international law and for total disarmament under world law. The reader or seminar participant is invited to weigh these alternative proposals against the world as it is and to consider the feasibility of constructing a more satisfactory world system.

FOR INDIVIDUAL READING, INFORMAL DISCUSSION OR SEMINAR

The following essays are structured for individual reading, for informal group discussion, or for more formal study and discussion in the tradition of the academic seminar.

INDIVIDUAL READING.

This book may be treated as a collection of nine essays or chapters, each dealing with a particular "cluster" of related problems in international affairs. The reader who is anxious to pursue any of these problems in depth is urged to follow the reading suggestions and references at the end of each essay. The thoughtful reader will also find the questions at the end of each chapter provocative and helpful in clarifying his own opinions.

INFORMAL DISCUSSION.

Any concerned citizen can very easily set up an informal home discussion group based on these materials. The first step is to invite a few interested friends, neighbors, couples or fellow club-members to set aside a convenient one or two hours a week for group discussion—one session for each of the nine sections in this book. The group may get together in a home or other convenient meeting place, or meetings can be rotated among the homes of the participants. Each participant (or couple) should purchase a copy of this book.

All that is required for constructive discussion is that each participant read the background essay *before* coming to the discussion session. The discussion should be based on the suggested questions at the end of each essay. These questions are designed to challenge individual opinions and to provoke discussion. Any member of the group may act as discussion leader, or the job may be rotated from week to week. (It is not necessary to use a trained discussion leader. In fact, an informal discussion may prove more instructive as well as more enjoyable.) As a variation on this pattern, the group may invite a local legal or political expert, journalist, economist or other specialist to lead or sit in on an occasional discussion session.

Seminar.

This volume is also designed to serve as the basis for a nine-session seminar, to be conducted on or off campus, in a regular or an extension division of an academic institution. In a formal seminar the instructor will normally assign additional reading beyond this volume. The suggested questions at the end of each session may be useful in structuring the seminar discussions.

SPECIAL PURCHASE ARRANGEMENTS

As a service to seminars and discussion groups, additional copies of this book may be ordered direct from the Fund for Education at $1.25 each for one to four copies, or at $1 each for five or more copies.

Also, quantity discounts are available for two titles which recur frequently in the reading lists for this seminar: *Legal and Political Problems of World Order,* an anthology of contemporary readings compiled and edited by Saul H. Mendlovitz ($2.25 for single copies) and *World Peace Through World Law,* by Grenville Clark and Louis B. Sohn ($2.50 for single copies). Orders and requests for further information should be addressed to the Fund for Education Concerning World Peace Through World Law, 11 West 42d Street, New York 36, N.Y. Checks, made out to *Fund for Education* must accompany all purchase orders.

SUGGESTIONS FOR DISCUSSION LEADERS

Anyone leading a discussion based on these materials will find it helpful to bear in mind the following points:

Constructive discussion does *not* have to end in consensus or agreement. There is wide room for honest disagreement. The discussion leader should therefore limit carefully the time spent on each question and then move the group on to another topic or problem.

A lively and rewarding discussion is one in which every member of the group takes some part. A good discussion leader can encourage this. One way is to ask the views of someone who has been too shy to speak up. Another way is to give all a chance to speak by interrupting, tactfully, someone who monopolizes the discussion.

The discussion leader should *not* do most of the talking. In an informal group or a formal academic seminar, the leader — or instructor — stimulates, encourages and may even guide discussion but he does not dominate it. Good discussion is a constructive exchange of ideas. This is very different from a lecture or a question-and-answer session.

A good discussion leader can do a number of things to add depth to the experience. These extras include being fully familiar with the background essay and suggested readings, deciding ahead of time what question or set of questions to use to launch a lively discussion, and starting and ending each session at the agreed hours.

SUGGESTIONS FOR DISCUSSION PARTICIPANTS

The most important investment an individual participant can make is to be familiar with the assigned material in advance of each meeting. This means reading the background essay for that session and, if time permits, perusing some of the additional readings suggested for the session.

The next most important advice to a discussion group participant is to speak up — and to give all other members of the group the opportunity to do the same.

And finally, if a participant finds the seminar a rewarding experience, he should consider how he may share the experience with others, by suggesting seminars in his church or other organizations he belongs to, by organizing a new seminar group himself.

THE CHALLENGE AND THE RESPONSIBILITY

If our free society is to marshal its wisdom and power to meet the challenges of the future, an alert and informed citizenry must shoulder the major burden. The first task is for the citizens to be familiar with the nature of the problems and alternative solutions. Only then can they make a responsible decision as to what national policies they will support or oppose.

This study is intended as a contribution to that process.

PEACE: THE CONTROL OF NATIONAL POWER

NATION-STATES HAVE HISTORICALLY CONSIDERED
it their sovereign right to use force — or threaten to use it — in support
of national aims and interests. Recent generations, however, have tried
by convention and treaty to limit or curtail the exercise of national
power. The United Nations Charter, for example, exacts a specific
pledge from all member nations to "refrain . . . from the threat or use
of force. . . ." Despite this pledge, and despite growing world-wide recognition that a major thermonuclear war would be disastrous, competitive military power remains a vital governing factor in international politics. The nation-state system continues to operate, in a fundamental
sense, as a "war system."

Attempts to move the world *away* from war are, in effect, attempts
to transform this war system into a "peace system." The goal of most
such proposals is to reduce the dangers of thermonuclear disaster by providing effective alternatives, other than war, for resolving disputes between nations. The common assumption is that nations and peoples will
continue to differ and to compete. The common hope, in this age of
almost instantaneous destruction, is that international competition may
take other forms than war.

Steps leading to a peace system may call for stabilization of the
arms race, or controlled reduction of armaments, or complete disarmament, or political and legal processes that will provide substitutes for war.
Or the proposals may imply fundamental changes in the whole structure
of international relations: a complete overhaul of the traditional prerogatives of national sovereignty and national military power. The major
test of the workability of a peace-system proposal is whether it can, simultaneously, (a) safeguard legitimate interests of peoples and nations and

(b) provide for peaceful settlement of disputes arising from competing national interests.

This seminar is concerned with precisely these problems: how the present international system operates, and the nature and feasibility of various proposed alternatives to the present system. In this first session you will explore three basic elements of the challenge:

1. The role of force (and deterrence) in today's world, as illustrated by the Cuban missile crisis of October-November 1962 and other recent events.

2. How the contemporary power system operates as nations rely on military power to pursue their aims and protect their interests.

3. Some basic alternative approaches to the control of national power and the creation of a more stable international system.

ELEMENTS IN THE CUBAN CRISIS

The Cuban missile crisis of October-November 1962 furnished a recent and vivid illustration of the chronic dangers inherent in a world political system which relies on competing military power.

The build-up to the crisis, during the summer and fall of 1962, was not the accumulating antagonisms between the United States and the Cuban government of Premier Fidel Castro. Rather it was the threat which the United States saw in the mounting influence of the Soviet Union in Cuba, especially the influx of Soviet "technicians" and military personnel and a growing arsenal of modern Soviet weapons. As summer gave way to autumn, the Soviet Union and the United States moved closer to direct confrontation. A central issue was the announced U. S. objective of a Cuba freed of Communist control and the announced Soviet objective of thwarting direct U. S. intervention in Cuba.

The crisis reached a head when the Soviet Union secretly introduced into Cuba a reported 42 missiles and 42 bomber aircraft capable of delivering nuclear explosives throughout most of the United States, southeastern Canada, all of Mexico, Central America and Panama, and northern South America. Upon verification of these facts by aerial reconnaissance, the United States mobilized a vast military striking force, including 300,-000 combat troops, 180 naval ships and hundreds of bomber, fighter and reconnaissance aircraft. A U. S. naval blockade of Cuba was set up and, according to some reports, 150 or more U. S. intercontinental ballistic missiles (ICBM's) were readied to hit targets in the Soviet Union. The United States demanded — and got — rapid withdrawal from Cuba of the Soviet offensive weapons that had been identified from the air.

NATURE OF THE THREAT

It is important to recognize the nature of the threat which, in Washington's view, Soviet nuclear weapons in Cuba represented. The strategic stakes help explain why the Soviet Union was willing to risk the consequences of being caught secretly introducing the weapons into Cuba while officially denying it had any intention of doing so. Similarly, the vigorous U.S. response is comprehensible only in terms of Washington's view of the specific threat.

Had Russia succeeded in making its weapons operational in Cuba, it would *not* have upset the world military balance of power, which is and would have remained in the U.S. favor. It would have acquired, however, an important temporary military advantage. Rockets launched from Cuba would have been able to by-pass the basic North American radar warning net, which is designed to detect an attack coming from the direction of the North Pole but not from the direction of the Caribbean. In addition, operational Russian missiles and bombers in Cuba would have greatly improved Russia's ability, in a first-strike attack, to knock out a significant number of U.S.-based missiles and bombers *on the ground*. (The warning time of a rocket attack from Cuba would be less than the fifteen minutes required to get U.S. Strategic Air Command — SAC — bombers into the air and slow-firing Atlas and Titan I missiles into trajectory.)

In a hypothetical U.S.-Soviet war in November 1962, Russia would have been able to offset, to an important degree, the vast U.S. lead in nuclear weapons. By moving into close range of U.S. missile and bomber bases, the Soviet Union would have been able (at the moment war broke out) to reduce the number of U.S. missiles and bombers available for a retaliatory blow against the Soviet Union. The U.S. weapons lead over the Soviet Union would not have been canceled out but would have been weakened.

Whether the Soviet Union contemplated attacking the United States, or hoped only to narrow the gap in strategic weapons, or sought some diplomatic and political leverage it might have gained with its Cuban missile and bomber bases, are unanswered questions. The weapons were forced out before they became operational.

In forcing the missile-bomber issue, the United States sacrificed, at least temporarily, its original objective—the elimination of communism and Soviet influence in Cuba. Indeed, substantial Soviet military personnel remained on the island, together with Soviet weapons classified as "defensive" — including high-altitude antiaircraft missiles, short-range rockets and coastal patrol boats. Moreover, U.S. military intervention in Cuba appeared to be ruled out for the indefinite future. On the showdown issue, however, the United States achieved its purpose: all visible Soviet offensive weapons capable of striking the territories of other American nations were removed. (A few observers suspect some Russian missiles may have been secreted in Cuban caves. The launching bases, however, were dismantled.)

CUBA: A TEST OF DETERRENCE

The U.S. lead over the Soviet Union in long-range missiles is sometimes estimated at five or six to one. In long-range bombers the United States is also known to have a considerable advantage. The Soviet attempt to set up missile and bomber bases in Cuba may have represented, at least in part, an effort to narrow this power gap. By issuing its ultimatum, the United States made clear it was willing to wage war at any level — from a brushfire campaign in Cuba to a global thermonuclear war—to prevent Russia from acquiring a significant offensive capability in Cuba.

By backing down and withdrawing its missiles and bombers, the Soviet Union implied it was *deterred* by relative U.S. military power in the Caribbean and by over-all U.S. military advantages in any all-out conflict.

If Russia had stood pat in Cuba, or had tried to run the U.S. naval blockade, the United States had ample conventional (non-nuclear) military force to wipe out the still unassembled missiles and bombers, occupy the Soviet bases and intercept Soviet relief or reinforcement efforts, whether by sea or air. In fact, the United States could no doubt have conquered and occupied all of Cuba without using any nuclear weapons (although at considerable cost in American, Russian and Cuban lives).

The Soviet Union could have "escalated" the crisis to the level of all-out thermonuclear war by launching a bomber and missile attack, from Russian territory, against an alerted United States. Even then the United States, with its great weapons superiority, would have been able to launch a devastating retaliatory blow on the Soviet Union, *even after the Russians had thrown their full military force into an attack on the United States.*

To the extent that Russia's decision to comply with the ultimatum was influenced by these power realities, Cuba was a demonstration of deterrence in operation — a situation in which one nation avoids or halts a particular action because it believes another nation is able and determined to prevent or punish the action.

LESSONS OF THE CUBAN CRISIS

In retrospect, the 14-day Cuban crisis of October-November 1962 illustrated the following characteristics of contemporary power politics:

1. POSSIBILITY OF WAR.

Thermonuclear war is "unthinkable" only in the sense that no nation can rationally expect "victory" unless it is willing to pay a price which, in any earlier age, would have been the cost of "defeat." Yet, in any clash in which the vital interests of the United States and the Soviet Union are at stake, war between the two superpowers (and, as a possible by-product, world war) can break out. Had Russia chosen to defy the U.S. ultimatum, major war could have resulted. Had the United States demanded more than Russia was willing to give—for example, immediate withdrawal of *all* Soviet personnel and weapons— Moscow might have felt obliged to fight in spite of its unfavorable military position. War could also have resulted from miscalculation, by either side, of the other's intentions or determination.

2. ROLE OF DETERRENCE.

There are also factors operating in the system which help avert war between the two superpowers. One of these, so far, is the rational desire on both sides to prevent a holocaust if possible. Another is the facts of relative military power in a given crisis situation—whether the military balance is heavily one-sided. Still another is whether the specific, usually limited objective in a given situation is worth the risk of total war. Finally, there is the question of credibility—whether the nation which has the initiative believes the other nation will go to war to arrest that initiative. It is questionable, for example, whether Russia would have complied with the U.S. ultimatum in Cuba if Moscow had not been convinced that the United States was willing to go "all the way" to total war to get Soviet offensive weapons out of Cuba. With all these factors operating, deterrence works and war is averted. In effect, deterrence operates when one nation puts the price-tag of "war" on a particular provocative action and thus deters another nation from committing the provocation.

3. PRECARIOUSNESS OF DETERRENCE.

Perhaps the most important lesson of the Cuban crisis is that, while deterrence has worked—in Cuba and probably in prior crisis situations —it is a precarious keeper of the peace. The world can come very close to the brink of war before one side or the other "blinks." The Soviet Union risked war by bringing its missiles and bombers into Cuba in the first place; the United States risked war by demanding their withdrawal. While neither side, deliberately sought armed conflict, the opportunities for war were numerous—through miscalculation, accident, political (as well as military) misjudgment, or by a spasm response to some sudden and threatening development such as the sinking of a Russian or U.S. ship on the blockade line.

The Cuban crisis demonstrated, in summary, that major war involving thermonuclear weapons is possible when the superpowers clash over what they consider to be their respective vital interests; that the fear of precipitating an unwanted war may deter a nation from risking a provocative action; but that nations will take enormous risks to improve their own strategic advantage or to prevent a potential enemy from doing so. Cuba also demonstrated that, under some circumstances, one superpower or the other may be willing to go to war because it feels its security threatened by the existence of particular kinds of weapons in a specific place.

IF DETERRENCE FAILS

In a competitive power sytem, accidental war is always a possibility. A false alarm, a human or mechanical error, a misreading of a potential enemy's intentions, even the unauthorized behavior of a military commander, may trigger a chain of events that gets completely out of hand in this age of quick-response weapons. (The United States — and hopefully other countries — is taking elaborate precautions against accident or unauthorized behavior in the control of nuclear weapons.)

In addition, a limited war (as in South Vietnam) may escalate into a major conflict — through miscalculation by either side. The risks of suprise defeat may appear too grave, in some situations, to allow for a calm and measured response to a sudden crisis. There is also the possibility of catalytic war—a war triggered by an ambitious or desperate third nation and soon joined by the superpowers out of fear, mistrust, or miscalculation. Such a war could conceivably be initiated by Cuba, East or West Germany, Communist China or the Republic of China, or some other lesser power.

Finally it is important to recognize that major war could be launched without warning as a deliberate calculation because, in some future clash of vital interests, one nuclear-armed power decided that war was the *least unfavorable* alternative it faced. The destructiveness of modern weapons, and the probability of retaliation, would weigh heavily in any such decision. However, the ultimate criterion would presumably be, Will the nation be better off after the exchange of nuclear blows than it is now, or than it would be if it did not initiate the war? The decision would be particularly poignant if the only alternatives appeared to be war or surrender.

'STABILIZED DETERRENCE'

A number of experts feel that the way out of the present dangerous situation is for the two superpowers to move in the direction of "stabilized deterrence" — a kind of mutual deterrent balance that would make the current arms race unnecessary.

Technologically, some stabilization of nuclear deterrence may already be on its way, as both sides acquire increasing numbers of highly invulnerable retaliatory (second-strike) weapons. In mid-December 1962, for example, the U.S. solid-fuel Minuteman missile became operational. The Minuteman is a relatively invulnerable weapon (buried in the ground in 80-foot silos) and is rapid-firing (32 seconds from command). It would take an almost direct hit from an H-bomb to destroy one of these buried and protected — "hardened" — missiles. Even a close range attack (as from Cuba), with barely a few minutes warning time, would not prevent a substantial proportion of these weapons from being launched in a retaliatory (second-strike) attack. Given any warning at all, most could be launched into trajectory before the Cuban-based missiles reached their targets; those retaliatory missiles remaining in their silos would survive all but direct hits.

U.S. deterrent power is becoming increasingly dependent on Minuteman, along with a growing armory of similarly invulnerable Titan II missiles and globally dispersed, submarine-based Polaris missiles. The Soviet Union is known to be acquiring comparable weapons. Thus the time may be near when *both* sides will have quantities of mutually invulnerable retaliatory weapons. This means *either* side may soon be able to sustain a sneak attack and still have enough retaliatory power left over to launch a devastating second strike on the aggressor.

The chief benefits of a stabilized deterrence system might be (a) a slow-down in today's frenetic arms race and (b) a reduced danger of either deliberately calculated nuclear aggression or accidental war.

A slow-down in the arms race might be possible if both sides decided to rely on adequate but limited numbers of invulnerable retaliatory weapons for security against surprise nuclear attack. The danger of such an attack might be reduced because no aggressor could hope to escape punishment—major retaliation would be a virtual certainty.

As a result, the danger of accidental war might also be reduced. Invulnerable deterrents would give both sides more time to react to sudden apparent threats; spasm responses would be unnecessary because, even if the threat proved real, the power to retaliate would still be secure. For example, in the event of a serious incident such as the unauthorized or accidental firing of a few missiles, the victim or target nation could afford to delay its response for a few minutes or even hours until it was sure the attacks were intentional and would continue. Only then would it launch its own full retaliatory power, plunging the two nations into maximum mutual destruction.

To summarize, the lopsided deterrence that apparently operated in the Cuban crisis was accident-prone in the sense that neither side could have afforded to delay an attack if it had become convinced that war was unavoidable. Had the United States reached this conclusion, it would have had much to gain by striking first. With its overwhelming weapons superiority it could have seriously crippled Russia's retaliatory power and thus minimized the amount of damage Russia could inflict on the United States in a second strike. Knowing this, the Soviet Union might have been tempted to strike first in order to destroy as many U.S. weapons as possible and thus reduce somewhat the destruction of its own territory. With both sides poised for total war, and each trying to second-guess the other, the opportunities for misstep and miscalculation were enormous. Deliberate clarity and restraint in the crisis negotiations were necessary in order to buy time, adjust bargaining positions, work out settlement terms, and begin the first measured steps back from the brink.

By contrast, a more symmetrical mutual deterrence system — stabilized deterrence — would presumably be less accident-prone for the reason that it would be difficult for either nation to believe that the other would deliberately launch a nuclear attack in the face of certain retaliation. Indeed, if the standoff in nuclear weaponry had been genuine in 1962, the Soviet Union might have felt no need to risk introducing strategic armaments into Cuba in the first place.

HOW MUCH STABILITY?

By definition, however, stabilized nuclear deterrence involves three characteristics which, in the long run, may lead to *less* rather than *more* stability in the international competition:

NUCLEAR STALEMATE AND CONVENTIONAL WAR.

Stabilized nuclear deterrence implies a standoff in nuclear weapons and delivery systems. This in itself may be difficult to achieve on mutually acceptable terms. The United States has already demonstrated, in Cuba, in successive rounds of nuclear testing, and in its growing arms budgets, that it has no intention of allowing the Soviet Union to approach military parity. The Soviet Union has demonstrated, in these same three areas, that it has no intention of abandoning its efforts to catch up. The effect of this conflict in purpose had been to heighten rather than moderate the arms race.

Assuming, however, that a more or less stable "balance of nuclear terror" were to emerge from the new and highly invulnerable weapons systems now being adopted, still another problem would emerge. A slow-down or stalemate in the nuclear arms race would automatically magnify the importance of non-nuclear or conventional weapons. Reducing the likelihood of thermonuclear war could multiply the danger of major war at the conventional level — in the style of World War II prior to Hiroshima or the Korean War.

In fact, most American and West European specialists who welcome the advent of stabilized nuclear deterrence also strongly advocate a build-up in U.S. and Allied conventional forces. Their aim is to match what are now numerically superior Communist bloc conventional forces and to provide the West with flexible alternatives to nuclear war — from full-scale conventional war capabilities for the defense of key areas (other than Western Europe, where tactical or battlefield nuclear weapons would almost certainly be used) to guerrilla and counterguerrilla capabilities in the jungles and hills of Southeast Asia and Latin America.

In short, a brief experience with stabilized deterrence at the nuclear level might soon lead to a crash arms race at the conventional level. Moreover, at some stage in a headlong conventional arms race, with a vital clash of interest at stake, one or both sides might suddenly resume the nuclear arms race in an effort to break the so-called nuclear stalemate.

BREAKING THE STALEMATE.

Even in a period of relatively stable nuclear deterrence, there is always the possibility of a technological breakthrough of such magnitude that the side which achieved it first would momentarily be in a position to overwhelm or cancel out the effectiveness of the other side's retaliatory power. In political terms, this would allow the side achieving the breakthrough to demand surrender or otherwise to impose its will on the other side.

There are a number of fields in which breakthroughs of this calibre are conceivable. Efficient antimissile missiles, capable of destroying a very high percentage of *second*-strike missiles while they were still en route to their targets, would make a *first* strike far less risky than at present. Particularly if combined with an efficient civil-defense system, an antimissile missile would tend to cancel out the other side's deterrent power and thus destabilize the mutual deterrence system.

Various imaginable "fantastic" weapons also have the potential, theoretically, of taking the stability out of stabilized deterrence. These include armed orbiting satellites or orbital launching platforms with extremely precise aiming accuracy, various possible applications of the laser or other "death ray" devices, and the multitudinous potentialities of biological, chemical and radiological warfare.

In other words, the era of stabilized deterrence which the United States and the Soviet Union appear to be entering can lead to increased instability in the non-nuclear aspects of the arms race and may be only temporarily stable at the nuclear level.

BILATERAL DETERRENCE IN A MULTILATERAL WORLD.

Finally, the concept of stabilized deterrence is limited, at this stage in history, to the mutual invulnerability of the retaliatory forces of the two superpowers—the United States and the Soviet Union. It is a bilateral or bipolar concept. It has little or nothing to do with the power competition—political and military—among other nations.

In the first place it overlooks the possible spread of nuclear power to other nations — the Nth country problem — in the absence of an effective universal ban on all nuclear testing. The test-ban treaty negotiated in Moscow in July 1963 does not prohibit underground tests, contains no enforcement provisions and applies only to those nations that voluntarily accede to it. In addition to Communist China (which has denounced the treaty) and France (which already has nuclear capabilities and intends to develop a national nuclear striking force), there are perhaps a dozen other nations with the technological capacity to acquire nuclear weapons in the near future. If nuclear weapons do proliferate, even on a relatively small scale, the international military climate could become so unstable that any U.S.-Soviet nuclear standoff would be irrelevant. The two superpowers could find themselves involved against their will in a "small" nuclear war initiated by another power, ally or neutral. Such a conflict could catalyze all-out nuclear hostilities on a global scale.

In the second place, the concept of bipolar deterrence — a U.S.-Soviet nuclear stalemate — greatly oversimplifies the complex power structure of the present international system. Despite the great power gap that divides the two superpowers from all other nations, world politics does not operate on a simply bipolar pattern. There are various levels of national power. The ways in which they combine and interact help determine the stability — or instability — of the system.

THE POWER SYSTEM IN OPERATION

The contemporary power system has four fundamental characteristics:

SUPERPOWER CONFRONTATION.

The dominant and perhaps decisive competition now going on in the world is between the two superpowers. U.S. and Soviet global aims are in direct conflict—ideologically, politically, socially, economically and militarily. The two military establishments are locked in a bilateral arms race in which the alliance systems on both sides play a secondary military role, although the political, economic and geographical importance of allies or satellites to both superpowers is incalculable. The respective alliance systems augment (and sometimes handicap) the exercise of super power on both sides; but, so far, only the United States and the Soviet Union are capable of deliberately taking the world into total thermonuclear war.

Relations between the superpowers — direct and indirect — tend to be regulated and modified by this fact. Neither side wants to risk total war if it can be avoided; both superpowers act as if they believe they can advance their aims and protect their interests without total war. The national security of both superpowers rests primarily on the determination of both sides to compete within certain unwritten and ill-defined rules. These include, for example, the avoidance of a direct armed clash between U.S. and Soviet military personnel — whether in Cuba, Berlin or Korea. The rules do *not* exclude clashes in which one superpower or the other is represented by the troops of a third or "proxy" nation — as in Korea, where Communist Chinese "volunteers" battled U.S. and other UN forces, or in South Vietnam, where U.S. military "advisers" participate directly in the struggle against South and North Vietnamese Communist guerrillas.

LESSER-POWER COMPETITION.

Under the umbrella of this superpower confrontation, the lesser powers (including allies on each side, such as Britain and France, China and Cuba) enjoy some latitude in the pursuit of old-fashioned power politics. There are "neighborhood" arms races in the Middle East, South Asia, Africa and (decreasingly so) in Latin America. Relative military power and force, or the threat of it, influence small-power diplomacy throughout the world—India and Portugal over Goa and the other Portuguese enclaves, India and Pakistan over Kashmir, Indonesia and the Netherlands over West Irian (West New Guinea), Indonesia and Malaya over the formation of the Federation of Malaysia, the United Arab Republic and Saudi Arabia over the civil war in Yemen, the Dominican Republic and Haiti over the principles of political asylum and diplomatic immunity, and so on.

REGULATING ROLE OF THE SUPERPOWERS.

An important regulating factor in the competition among lesser powers is universal recognition that the superpowers are unlikely to allow any "local" conflict to inflate to the proportions where it may explode as a showdown issue between the superpowers themselves. Since super military power is in the hands of only two nations, all other nations are relatively limited in their ability to defend themselves from major attack. For a few of these nations the threshold of self-reliance is fairly high—Britain, with substantial conventional power and a modest nuclear striking capability; France, with modern conventional forces and the bare beginnings of nuclear capabilities; Communist China with massive conventional power; Sweden and Switzerland, with elaborate underground civil defense installations and formidable self-defense forces that would take a heavy toll of any invader, even a nuclear-armed invader intent on occupying (rather than obliterating) either country.

Yet for all lesser powers—Britain and France, as well as Sweden and Switzerland, or Japan or Israel or Venezuela—national security *ultimately* depends on the ability and willingness of one or both superpowers to intervene on their behalf, or to contain or suppress any dangerous local hostilities.

In a sense, therefore, and only to a degree, the lesser powers can afford some recklessness in their power politics *because* their security—or rather, any serious threat to the stability of the international system—is of direct concern to the competing superpowers. To a very real extent, the superpowers set the limits of tolerance on conflicts involving the lesser powers, including their own allies.

INTERACTION BETWEEN POWER LEVELS.

There is also a complex interplay between power levels. It is a process which sometimes imposes restraints on the actions of the superpowers. Under other circumstances the interplay opens up opportunities for either or both superpowers to capitalize on a local conflict and to try to manipulate it in favorable directions.

If a brushfire war poses no real threat to the interests of either the United States or the Soviet Union, and is obviously not a threat to the general peace, the superpowers may not intervene at all—even if there is a formal military alliance which provides technical grounds for intervention. The United States, for example, made no move to aid its NATO ally, Portugal, when India marched on Portuguese Goa and other enclaves on the Indian subcontinent.

If a brushfire conflict does threaten superpower interests, or the general peace, a superpower may intervene in an unusual way. In 1962 when war over West Irian seemed a possibility between Soviet-equipped Indonesia and the Netherlands, a U.S. ally in NATO, the United States applied diplomatic pressure on the Netherlands to accept a settlement which gave the Indonesians virtually everything they asked. (The settlement was labeled a compromise since it involved a brief transition, under UN authority, from Dutch to Indonesian sovereignty and, technically, a later plebiscite by the people of West Irian.) In this instance, the United States was apparently less concerned with the merits of the conflicting territorial claims of the two lesser powers than with the long-term political consequences of the dispute. Indonesia's pivotal role in Southeast Asia imposed certain pressures and restraints on U.S. policy.

The border conflict between India and Communist China produced an even more complex interplay between power levels. When there appeared to be some real danger that ill-prepared Indian troops might be overrun by Communist Chinese forces, the United States (and Britain) responded to Indian requests with immediate and substantial military aid. Some Soviet military aid also arrived in India during the border fighting, although the quantity and timing of the shipments suggested that Moscow's purpose was more political and psychological than military. While the threat of superpower intervention may have had no effect on subsequent Communist Chinese policy, the event nonetheless demonstrated that when war breaks out at the lesser-power level the great powers, especially the superpowers, are usually concerned and may intervene to halt the conflict or to try to influence its course.

In some situations, one superpower or the other (or both) considers it advantageous to its own long-range interests to encourage or manipulate a conflict between smaller powers, or to intervene directly (or indirectly, by proxy) in a small-power conflict to influence the outcome of the struggle. The civil war in Laos is an example. U.S. advisers and military aid backed one faction while another faction received Soviet supplies, Communist Chinese equipment and advisers and Communist North Vietnamese troop support. Similarly, U.S. government agencies have, in the past, assisted an anti-Communist revolution in Guatemala (1954) and an unsuccessful Cuban-exile invasion and subsequent exile raids against Castro Cuba (1961-62). In these same operations, the Soviet Union was aiding the opposition.

Finally, the lesser powers are occasionally successful in deliberately imposing certain restraints on the actions of one or both superpowers. The UN is the usual forum for doing so and the technique is most successful when it involves small-power mediation in a superpower deadlock. During the Cuban missile crisis, the nonpermanent members of the Security Council were influential both in delaying a showdown vote (which became unnecessary when Moscow finally admitted the presence of its missiles in Cuba and agreed to withdraw them) and in keeping open backstage channels of mediation between Moscow and Washington. (The crisis was finally resolved, however, in direct exchanges of corre-spondence between President Kennedy and Chairman Khrushchev.)

Small-power influence is also an important factor in the OAS. Latin America's deep antipathy to U.S. intervention in the affairs of its neighbors undoubtedly influences U.S. policy toward Cuba. It was perhaps a factor in the absence of open U.S. combat support for the Cuban exiles in the 1961 Bay of Pigs invasion and has tended to limit U.S. freedom of action since then.

CONTROL OF NATIONAL POWER

This complex and interacting power system is characteristic of a world in which (a) two hostile nations share a monopoly of super military power and are locked in a spiraling arms race, while (b) other nations, whatever their threshold of self-reliance, are engaged in tests of force, and arms competition, in pursuit of their own interests.

The stability of the system depends on competitive military factors such as deterrence, on the one hand, and on the other hand, on the restraint which nations large and small are willing to exercise in their use of power—their willingness to conform to the system's uncertain and unwritten rules.

Understandably, therefore, much of the contemporary debate on problems of international peace and stability focuses on the question of how to control the military aspect of national power. Broadly speaking, there are three general approaches to this question:

1. ARMS CONTROL.

This is a very wide category of proposals intended to modify, adjust or stabilize the arms race, or moderate the tensions arising from the arms race. The proposals include such limited or first-step measures as a nuclear test-ban, reciprocal measures to reduce the danger of surprise attack, agreements to ban certain weapons, the denuclearization or demilitarization of certain sensitive geographical areas, or simply open acceptance on both sides of stabilized deterrence—with or without some safeguards. Some arms control proposals call for far more exten- sive measures such as a comprehensive treaty on the reduction of all types of armaments, together with inspection machinery and perhaps penalties and enforcement measures.

2. GENERAL AND COMPLETE DISARMAMENT.

Proposals for general and complete disarmament (also called com- prehensive or universal disarmament) are designed to deprive all nations of their traditional sovereign prerogative to use force in support of national aims and interests. National military forces would be reduced, by universal agreement, to the level of impotence for aggressive purposes. (Various proposals differ, however, on how much reduction of military strength would be necessary to insure impotence.) General and complete disarmament has political as well as military implications: it foreshadows, not just a change in climate, but also a change in terrain. To eliminate national armaments is to wipe out the foundations of the present world power system. Therefore, some disarmament proposals call for the creation of global institutions (or a strengthened UN) which would have sufficient military power to enforce disarmament and peace.

3. GENERAL AND COMPLETE DISARMAMENT UNDER
   WORLD LAW.

The most comprehensive proposals for universal disarmament go still further. They call for the creation of a global authority (or greatly strengthened UN) which would have a complete monopoly on military power and would, in addition, contain machinery for the peaceful resolution of international disputes and for the enforcement of disarmament and peace under world law. The intent is not simply to remove the most serious dangers characteristic of the contemporary war system; it is also to provide the framework and institutions for a wholly new peace system.

MODEL OF A WORLD 'PEACE SYSTEM'

There are various proposals for transforming the present world system into a more stable community through disarmament under some measure of enforceable world law. The most extensive proposal is the Clark-Sohn plan set forth in one of the suggested readings for this seminar, the book *World Peace Through World Law*.

This plan is a useful one to study for several reasons. It attempts to deal with the root causes of war as well as with the arms race. At the same time, it attempts to provide checks, balances, inducements and limitations which its authors believe would make the total plan politically acceptable to all sides. It is also a detailed plan, suggesting specific modifications to the present UN charter. As such, it is perhaps the most comprehensive existing "model" of a disarmed world under law.

Whether the Clark-Sohn proposals are in themselves politically realistic, or likely of adoption, is less important than that they detail the complex problems and opportunities inherent in the present power system and the elaborate measures which may be required to manage this complexity.

Minimum essentials of the Clark-Sohn plan include the following:

Clark and Sohn argue that general and complete disarmament is one of the essential preconditions for world peace and stability. They suggest that the world should accept an enforceable universal law against the use or threat of force in international relations. This implies certain other minimum essentials, including the following:

1. It would be necessary to establish "an adequate world police force in order that, after complete disarmament has been accomplished, the means will exist to deter or apprehend violators of the world law" forbidding national armaments and international violence.

2. Simultaneously, it would be essential to set up "alternative peaceful means to deal with all disputes between nations"—that is, some kind of world judicial and conciliation system.

3. Further, "in the interest of a solid and durable peace," it would be strongly advisable to set up some kind of world development authority to reduce the dangerous disparities in wealth between the "have" and "have-not" nations.

All these measures, in turn, according to Clark and Sohn, are unattainable in any practical sense without three important structural changes in the present world system:

1. "A world legislature with carefully limited yet adequate power to vote the annual budgets of the world peace authority . . . , to enact appropriate penalties for violation of the world law and other essential regulations concerning disarmament and the maintenance of peace, and to keep a watchful eye on the other organs and agencies of the peace authority."

2. "A world executive, free from any crippling veto, . . . to direct and control the world inspection service and the world police force and to exercise other essential executive functions" in the limited area of war prevention.

3. "An effective world revenue system" to support these supranational institutions on a reliable and continuing basis.

The significance of the Clark-Sohn approach is that each step and each measure in the plan is seen as an interdependent part of a new world system. The proposed peace authority would have carefully defined powers under limited world law—it would operate only in the area of maintaining peace. All other powers would still be reserved to nations and their peoples. Yet the limited job of maintaining peace, according to Clark and Sohn, would require radical departures from the present international system.

LOOKING AHEAD

The problem (and you will encounter it frequently in the course of this seminar) is to decide what approaches are both desirable and feasible—what kind of world do we want to live in and what kind can we, in practical terms, construct? Is it possible to pursue our peaceful goals, and to avoid a major war, by making some changes in the present international "war system"? Or are there compelling reasons for setting out to construct a wholly new "peace system"?

SUGGESTED READINGS:

MENDLOVITZ, *Legal and Political Problems of World Order* NY: Fund for Education, 1963, pp. 9-75.

CLARK AND SOHN, *World Peace Through World Law.* 2d edition. Cambridge: Harvard, 1962, pp. xv-xvii, 206-213.

ADDITIONAL READINGS:

HERZ, JOHN H. "The Rise and Demise of the Territorial State." *World Politics* 9: 473-493 (July, 1957).

KENNAN, GEORGE F. "Peaceful Coexistence: A Western View." *Foreign Affairs* 38: 171-190 (Jan. 1960).

KHRUSHCHEV, NIKITA S. "On Peaceful Coexistence." *Foreign Affairs* 38: 1-18 (Oct. 1959).

WASKOW, ARTHUR I. "The Limits of Defense." *Atlantic Monthly* 209: 80-98 (Feb. 1962).

REFERENCES:

COUSINS, NORMAN. *In Place of Folly.* NY: Harpers, 1961.

CLAUDE, INIS L., JR. *Swords Into Plowshares, The Problems and Progress of International Organization.* NY: Random House, 1956.

ETZIONI, AMITAI. *The Hard Way to Peace: A New Strategy.* NY: Collier, 1962.

HERZ, JOHN H. *International Politics in the Atomic Age.* NY: Columbia University Press, 1959.

KAHN, HERMAN. *Thinking About the Unthinkable.* NY: Horizon, 1962.

MILLIS, WALTER, AND JAMES REAL. *The Abolition of War.* NY: Macmillan, 1963.

MORGENTHAU, HANS. *Politics Among Nations.* 3rd edition. NY: Knopf, 1960.

STRACHEY, JOHN. *On the Prevention of War.* NY: St. Martin's, 1962.

Session I.   QUESTIONS FOR REFLECTION OR DISCUSSION

1. What are the prospects for war in our time?

Looking at the present world scene, and trends under way, what do you think are the prospects that a major thermonuclear war will break out by 1985?

If you think such a war is *likely,* how do you think it might break out? Which countries would probably be participants? How might such a war end and what might the aftereffects be?

If you think major thermonuclear war is *unlikely* between now and 1985, what factors do you think will help prevent it? Do you envision any important change in the arms race, for example? Or some significant political changes in the world community?

Do you think that "small" wars, without thermonuclear weapons, may be likely between now and 1985? If so, on how big a scale—as destructive as World War II? Or the Korean war?

2. *What role does deterrence perform in the contemporary power system?*

Do you think deterrence operated in the Cuban missile crisis? If so, in what way? Does it operate in Berlin? Taiwan? Laos? If you feel deterrence does not operate in these areas, what has so far prevented war in each case? Can we count on any or all of these factors to continue to prevent war during, say, the next decade?

What are the chances that "stabilized deterrence" can maintain peace during the next decade?

3. *What role does the UN perform in the contemporary power system?*

How important do you think the UN was in the peaceful resolution of the Cuban missile crisis? Should it, or could it have played a larger role? If so, how? Is there such a thing as a "world interest" which was or should have been represented in the Cuban crisis? If so, what is it and who represents it?

What various roles does the UN play in the world power system? Are there other roles it should play?

4. *How does the world power system really operate?*

Do you disagree in any way with the description of the world power system on pages 12-16? If so, what factors do you feel tend to "regulate" international affairs? What factors help prevent war? What factors make war possible or likely?

Are some new restraints on national power necessary if major wars are to be avoided? What restraints or controls do you feel are necessary or desirable? How do your views compare with the three approaches described on pages 16-17? with the Clark-Sohn model of a "world peace system"?

SUMMARY QUESTION:

Are there some values which you cherish more than peace, and for which would you be willing to go to war? What are these values? How secure are these values in the present competitive power system?

A VARIETY OF RAPID, REVOLUTIONARY CHANGES are under way in nearly every society on the face of the globe. There are simultaneous revolutions in science, technology and economics, in ideology and politics, in ethical outlook and social practice. These revolutions are fed by man's new insights into the material universe and into his own values and capacities. Changes are based on new skills and growing sources of capital, on rising demand and new and more effective ways of managing production and distribution. They lead to conflicting economic, social and political theories and systems. They affect the hopes and prospects of individuals and of nations.

The patterns of change overlap, reinforce each other and help create upheavals and conflicts *within* societies—between competing economic interests, majority and minority ethnic groups, and people of different political and ethical persuasions. They also give rise to cooperation, competition, tension and conflict *between* nations.

Domestic law performs an important function in helping to manage these changes within a society. In societies built on Western common law traditions in particular, the law is the principal mechanism for insuring nonviolent change that is equitable for all concerned. Working in concert with political institutions—legislatures and executive bodies—the courts attempt to protect private rights and interests against injustice, to arbitrate or decide disputes between conflicting interests, to interpret and apply legislation according to both the letter of the law and the traditional values of the society, to prevent violence on the part of citizens and arbitrary acts on the part of government, and to deter or punish departures from accepted standards.

In performing these functions, the law itself changes and is applied in new ways to meet fresh insights and changing conditions, as the history of civil rights in the United States demonstrates.

Law also performs important functions in the contemporary world of sovereign nation-states. International law, however, is far more limited and differs in fundamental respects from domestic law, particularly that body of international law which deals with restraints on the use or threat of force between nations. In addition, international law is almost exclusively concerned with relations among sovereign and independent nation-states, rather than with individuals.

In the previous session you examined the role of force in today's world. In this session you will explore the uses of law to control and prevent violence between nations. You will examine three aspects of the problem:

1. Scope and limitations of contemporary international law, including essential differences between domestic and international law.
2. Problems of making effective use of existing legal processes and institutions, especially the UN, in the contemporary world of power politics.
3. Alternative proposals for making existing international law more effective, for strengthening international law through UN Charter revision or other means, or for instituting some measure of enforceable world law operating under appropriate world institutions.

LAW IN TODAY'S WORLD

According to the late Secretary-General of the United Nations, Dag Hammarskjold, the world is "still in the transition between institutional systems of international coexistence and constitutional systems of international cooperation." There is a long road yet to be traveled, in other words, between an international law system which helps hostile nations to coexist and one which induces them to cooperate in their common interest.

In the present system, relations between nations tend to be regulated by a substantial body of recognized customs, procedures, rules and laws that have been built up over centuries of practice and formalization. There are even rules regulating the conduct of war—handling of prisoners, prohibition of certain kinds of weapons, definition of blockades and contraband, etc.

Some of these rules and practices—especially those which clearly serve the common interests of nations, as in commerce, communications and transportation—are systemized in formal agreements and reviewed and administered through a variety of international institutions such as the UN and various of its specialized agencies: International Telecommunications Union (ITU), International Postal Union (IPU), International Civil Aviation Organization (ICAO) and Intergovernmental Maritime Consultative Organization (IMCO). A vast body of rules, practices and multilateral commitments is embodied in treaties, conventions and informal agreements among nations or in the widespread observance of time-honored custom.

Some elements of international law have universal or near-universal acceptance, such as diplomatic immunity and rules of maritime commerce and navigation. Other elements of international law have more limited acceptance, such as right of political asylum and principle of dual citizenship. Still other matters are subject to continuing dispute, such as the right to expropriate foreign-owned property (and the conditions for doing so), freedom of passage in international waterways under national control (for example, the Suez Canal), and width of territorial seas.

Treaty law is technically binding only on the signatories to the treaty although treaties often embody principles or practices which already have or soon gain widespread or universal acceptance. Treaties may be revised, adjusted and even abrogated, however. Such changes may occur when there is a change in political conditions. The original objective of the treaty may no longer be possible or desirable. Or the bargaining power of one of the signatories may be enhanced sufficiently to demand and get a treaty revision.

International law in the contemporary world rests primarily on voluntary agreements among nations and on the pressures of custom, opinion, convenience and national self-interest that lie behind these voluntary agreements.

To understand the scope and limits of contemporary international law, and especially the problems of maintaining peace and stability under existing law and institutions, it will be helpful to examine certain contrasts between international and domestic law. These contrasts include the different ways in which these two types of law are enacted, applied and enforced.

ENACTMENT: SOURCES OF DOMESTIC AND INTERNATIONAL LAW

Domestic law in a highly developed modern nation may be said to flow "vertically" from a single sovereignty which, within the nation, has legally unlimited authority. In Britain this sovereignty rests technically with Parliament acting with the Queen. In the United States, the people are sovereign: through their elected representatives they indirectly enact the laws or amend the Constitution under which they live. In a totalitarian society the sovereign state or ruling party may govern by command, rather than legislation, but the flow of law is nonetheless vertical.

The institutions for a vertical flow do not now exist in the world community. Instead, the flow is "horizontal" among more than 120 sovereign and (formally, at least) equal states. Nations "enact" international law only when they agree to certain procedures, prohibitions and, perhaps, sanctions or penalties. They leave great vacuums in the law when they are unable to agree. There is no single global sovereignty empowered to legislate vertically or to command nations to conform to a single world body of law.

The most important example of this limitation is the UN, which (with 111 members in mid-1963) is the only nearly universal institution in existence. In framing the UN Charter, the founder-members delegated no significant legislative or command authority to the UN. The General Assembly is not a world parliament. Its powers are carefully limited to such functions as to "discuss," "consider," "make recommendations," "receive and consider reports," "initiate studies," "consider and approve the budget," elect members to other organs, admit new members, apportion expenses and establish subsidiary organs (Articles 10-17 and 22). Only the assessment or taxing power (Article 17) authorizes the General Assembly to enact a binding obligation, with penalties, on all members. (You will examine the special problems related to UN financing in Session IV.)

In the area of maintaining or restoring peace, the Security Council has primary responsibility and mandatory or binding powers under Chapter VII of the Charter. It is powerless to undertake an enforcement action, however, which any of the five permanent members— Britain, China, France, the Soviet Union or the United States—may oppose with a veto (Article 27). And, in the settlement of disputes which threaten the peace, the Security Council, like the General Assembly, has only the power of recommendation.

Furthermore, "Nothing contained in the present Charter shall authorize the United Nations to intervene in matters which are essentially within the domestic jurisdiction of any state or shall require the Members to submit such matters to settlement . . ." (Article 2, paragraph 7). The only exception is a case where the Security Council is empowered by the Charter—and unobstructed by veto—to act to maintain or restore peace (Articles 41 and 42).

The UN, in other words, cannot enact international law in the same sense that a sovereign nation can enact domestic law. In areas other than peace-enforcement the UN can only urge its sovereign members to observe its recommendations. Even in the vital area of maintaining peace, the UN's powers are limited by the veto and by the realities of power politics.

To summarize, contemporary international law comes into being through a horizontal (decentralized) rather than a vertical (centralized) process. It emerges from formal agreements among nations (treaties and conventions) or from informal agreements, tradition, consensus or widely accepted practice (customary international law).

APPLICATION: DOMESTIC VERSUS INTERNATIONAL LAW

Another distinguishing characteristic of international, as opposed to domestic, law is the way it is applied to specific disputes.

The primary function of a judiciary in a national legal system is the uniform, impartial and objective application of existing rules to decide a controversy. The international community, by contrast, lacks not only a genuine legislative process to enact law, it also lacks a judiciary with the independent power to apply the rules impartially and objectively whenever a dispute arises.

The International Court of Justice at the Hague (which has heard about fifty cases since 1946) has only as much jurisdiction as sovereign nations grant it. This voluntary submission to the Court's jurisdiction may be provided for automatically in a specific treaty, it may be granted by an individual nation in a general declaration of principle, or it may arise when two nations that are parties to a dispute agree in advance to accept the Court's jurisdiction and abide by its ruling.

The Court, one of the six principal organs of the UN, is not intended under the Charter to be the only medium for peacefully settling disputes. In addition, the Charter urges "negotiation, enquiry, mediation, conciliation, arbitration, . . . resort to regional agencies or arrangements, or other peaceful means. . . ." (Article 33).

The Charter also recognizes "the inherent right of individual or collective self-defense if an armed attack occurs against a Member of the United Nations, until the Security Council has taken measures necessary to maintain international peace and security" (Article 51). It was under this Article that the United States responded to Lebanon's request for military assistance during region-wide upheavals in the Middle East in 1958. Once the Security Council acted to establish a "presence" in Lebanon, U. S. assistance forces withdrew.

Finally, Chapter VIII of the UN Charter (Articles 52-54) recognizes "the existence of regional arrangements or agencies for dealing with such matters relating to the maintenance of international peace and security as are appropriate for regional action. . . ." The only provisos are that the activities of these regional bodies be "consistent with the Purposes and Principles of the United Nations" (Article 52, paragraph 1) and that the Security Council "at all times be kept fully informed" of these activities (Article 54). The Organization of American States (OAS), of all regional organizations, has acted most extensively within these Charter provisions. In 1961 and again in 1962, for example, the OAS voted to isolate Cuba within the hemisphere system and to support various (but not all) U. S. proposals designed to contain the threat of Cuban subversion in the rest of the hemisphere. In 1963 the OAS acted to settle peaceably a dispute between Haiti and the Dominican Republic.

The UN Charter recognizes, in other words, a variety of national and collective uses of power for the maintenance of peace in a world in which sovereign nations still rely on force to protect their interests. The Charter is silent on the question whether disputes settled in this fashion are necessarily settled "equitably." Lacking the instruments and authority for the uniform, impartial and objective application of existing rules or principles to decide a controversy, the UN leaves to the nation-states substantial responsibility for conflict-resolution by traditional means. Individual nations and group of nations, in turn, often act according to their own interpretation of international law. On occasions, when they have the power to do so, they may ignore or openly defy accepted interpretations of the law in enforcing a solution to a conflict.

The UN does not transform the existing power structure. Rather it reflects it and provides additional machinery—and pressure, without compulsion—to help the system work in a less war-prone way. The competitive power of sovereign nations to pursue or protect their own interests is still the ultimate factor in managing change in the world.

ENFORCEMENT: DOMESTIC VERSUS INTERNATIONAL LAW

The third major distinction between domestic and international law is the absence in the world community of a universal, permanent and effective enforcement agency comparable to domestic police.

The enforcement provisions of the UN Charter are contained in Chapter VII (Articles 39 through 51). This Chapter provides for various degrees of collective action, primarily through the UN, to meet "threats to the peace, breaches of the peace and acts of aggression." These collective measures range from mild sanctions to the use of armed force.

Police power to carry out these provisions was originally to have been made available to the Security Council by all member nations on a stand-by basis (Article 43). Negotiations setting up these on-call military units were never completed, however, because the great powers were unable to reach agreement on technical, let alone political, problems involved.

As a result, all past UN peace forces called into action—from Palestine to Yemen—have been *ad hoc* in nature. They have been recruited, not from all member nations, but from those nations that volunteered military units at the time of the crisis or from those nations which the Secretary-General considered politically appropriate for the specific operation. UN forces in Korea were volunteered by 16 member nations, including the United States and Britain, both major powers. UN forces in the Congo were recruited from small, primarily African, nations.

The peace-enforcement arm of the UN has never been set up on the universal stand-by basis provided for in the Charter. It is on these grounds that the Soviet Union considers all past peace-force operations of the UN to be "illegal" in the sense that they have been *ad hoc* in nature and have generally been recruited by the Secretary-General and supervised by the General Assembly, rather than recruited and supervised by the Security Council, the UN organ with primary responsibility for peace-enforcement. (You will explore the consequences of this issue in later sessions.)

To summarize once again, the existing body of international law is extensive and, generally speaking, tends to be observed as a matter of convenience or self-interest by the nations which subscribe to it, or simply for purposes of reciprocity—to induce other nations to observe the same restraints. In contrast with domestic law, however, the international community lacks institutions and effective procedures for enacting, applying and enforcing law on a uniform global basis. This condition is in part due to the depth of the conflicts in aims and interests among sovereign states, to the continuing reliance on relative national power to secure these aims and interests, and to the absence of any real consensus in the world community on what constitute legitimate national interests, desirable common interests, or acceptable rules and procedures for peacefully managing conflicts in national interest.

WHY DO NATIONS OBSERVE LAW?

The growth in the past century in international law offers ample evidence that nations recognize their stake in maintaining or even expanding a system of international law which is tolerable to them—the rules or principles which they consider right, convenient, protective or otherwise desirable. Furthermore, a nation habitually cites its understanding of international law to justify its own actions or to condemn the actions of other nations. Most nations prefer to maintain the image, at least, of respect for and conformity to international law.

This is understandable since a government wanting to violate a treaty or accepted rule of international law must always weigh the consequences of doing so. Defiance of international law may arouse vigorous domestic criticism of the government, particularly in an open society where the people have access to the important facts. Lawless action may also antagonize governmental or public opinion in other nations—allies, friends or neutrals—and may raise suspicion or other obstacles to achieving wholly unrelated foreign policy aims. Finally, lawlessness may invite retaliation from another country.

Theoretically no sovereign nation may deliberately wish to limit its own freedom of action. Yet any nation may be willing to do so *within tolerable limits* in order to impose similar restraints on the freedom of action of other nations.

BREAKDOWN OF INTERNATIONAL LAW

When international law breaks down, or is by-passed or ignored, the reasons may be various and complex. A government may decide that a law, rule or treaty is obsolete or unfair, or that it does not really apply in a specific case, or that the risk of lawlessness is less than the disadvantages of complying with the law. Or the government in question may have complete contempt for a particular body of international law and may believe it has the power to transcend it successfully.

There have been numerous examples, since World War II, when nations have successfully defied their treaty commitments (including their obligations under the UN Charter, which is, of course, a treaty among sovereign nations). Likewise, there are plenty of recent examples when nations have acted contrary to widely accepted principles of international law or independent of normal procedures and practices in international relations.

The enforced communization of Eastern Europe and the protracted division of Germany and Korea are in violation of formal agreements by the Soviet Union to support free elections in all these areas. The Anglo-French and Israeli invasions of Egypt in 1956 are generally considered to be violations of the pledge, under the Charter, to renounce force in pursuit of national aims. The unsuccessful U. S.-supported invasion of Cuba in April 1961 and the U. S. blockade and threat to use force against Russian missile and bomber bases in Cuba in October 1962 were both undertaken outside the provisions in the UN Charter for peaceful settlement of disputes. India's expulsion of the Portuguese from the enclaves of Goa, Damao and Diu in December 1961 involved the use of national force in lieu of the peaceful means for resolving international disputes called for in the UN Charter.

Yet in each of these cases, the "offending" nations justified their actions according to some legal principle or sovereign prerogative. In the case of Eastern Europe, the Soviet Union maintained that the Soviet-style elections and referendums held in these countries under Red Army supervision were democratic, that they fostered "progressive" (that is, Communist) forces in these societies and that they forestalled "imperialist" and "neo-Fascist" forces that would have set-up anti-Soviet regimes on Russia's borders.

Britain and France justified their invasion of Egypt on the grounds that Cairo's seizure of the foreign-owned Suez Canal was "illegal" and that all efforts at a just and peaceful resolution of the dispute had been exhausted. Israel justified its part in the campaign on national security grounds: it had been subjected to repeated border raids and claimed it had evidence of an imminent Egyptian attack; therefore Israel invaded the Gaza Strip and Sinai Peninsula in order to clean out raider bases and destroy armaments which Egypt was said to be stockpiling for aggression.

U. S. actions in support of anti-Castro Cuban exiles have been justified on the basis of past hemisphere (OAS) declarations that communism is an ideology alien to the region as well as on the basis of evidence that Castro was engaged in terrorism and subversive warfare against several Latin American nations. U. S. actions in the missile crisis (undertaken with full OAS support) were grounded on national, hemisphere and Western security.

Indian military action against the Portuguese enclaves in 1961 was widely deplored in Western capitals as an exercise of military force which was not only incompatible with India's pledges under the UN Charter, but also inconsistent with India's pretensions of morality in international relations. In New Delhi, Moscow and many capitals of the "new," former colonial states, however, India's action was viewed as legally justified liberation of Indian territory from the illegal colonial control of a European power.

Obviously these are conflicting views of international law, and of the order of priorities among various legal principles in a given situation. These differences can best be understood not by review of the law itself, but by analysis of the power politics involved—the conflicting aims and values of various nations and the reasons why particular international legal principles may be acceptable—or intolerable—to individual nations.

THREE VIEWS OF INTERNATIONAL LAW

Law, as you noted earlier, can be a mechanism for managing orderly change—within a national society or within a community of nations. In this sense, law participates in political change. When the dominant elements of a society want change in a particular direction, they may turn to law to authorize, specify, justify or regulate the change. Similarly, in the international community, nations tend to support those legal principles and rules which help "push" the world in directions they favor—or which discourage changes they consider unfavorable.

For purposes of illustration, it is possible to classify some of these conflicting attitudes into three groups.

1. WESTERN LEGAL TRADITIONS.

The foundations of contemporary international law are essentially Western in origin—the product of common Western European and North American traditions and values, and of an era when these cultures dominated or dictated the terms of international commerce, politics and diplomacy. Implicit in these traditions are legal guarantees for the rights of sovereign nations, of individuals and of private property. In an earlier age the Western powers were able to enforce observance of these rights by other nations—through political, economic or military pressure. With its coercive power reduced, the West seeks in the present age to extend and reinforce recognition of these rights through universal adoption of Western legal principles. It is seeking, in other words, to push the world in the direction of a rule of law that is compatible with Western traditions and values, as well as with Western security interests. Yet even among Western nations there are divergences in attitude toward such traditional principles as the self-determination of peoples, rights of foreign property-owners and still other issues which may, at a particular moment, conflict with national political interests.

2. INTERESTS OF EMERGING NATIONS.

The vast majority of the developing nations are former colonies or dependencies of Western powers. Most of them are nonwhite. All of them share certain common experiences. These include a long history of Western economic, if not political, domination and a strong, occasionally pathological, fear of external domination in any "modern" form— economic or political imperialism or colonialism. They also share mutual interests. Many of these nations suffer from what they consider to be unsatisfactory terms of trade with the industrialized (especially Western) nations, excessive foreign private control over domestic investment and natural resources, and an unjust disparity between their own national incomes and the wealth of those nations that have historically "exploited" them. Although most of the emerging nations have adopted Western political and juridical institutions and forms, some feel impelled, by nationalism or by the absence of an educated citizenry and viable economy, to adapt the rules and develop their own forms of political economy. In international law these nations tend to support principles which assure them maximum control over their own resources and foreign-owned property, minimum foreign interference, maximum draft on foreign assistance, immediate termination of all remaining colonial rule, immediate elimination in all other nations of all forms of discrimination against nonwhites and, finally, measures which may limit the military power of the major nations, reduce the danger of war and produce the stable peace which will provide the most advantageous conditions for their own progress. These nations, in other words, would like international law to help push the world in the direction best suited to their own values and their rapid modernization. They are not all in agreement, however, on the principles and rules of international law that will best serve these purposes.

3. Soviet view of international law.

The Soviet Union, also, is attempting to push the world in directions it favors. In classic Marxist-Leninist terms, the ultimate shape of the world is to be a single classless and stateless Communist society. In the transitional period, the Communist nations claim they are building their own forms of socialist law, which is wholly distinct from "bourgeois" or capitalist law and is "at all times determined by revolutionary necessity." International law in the transitional period—pending the victory of communism—is simply all those rules and principles which happen to be common to both capitalist and Communist practices. International organizations to which both sides belong can be nothing more, therefore, than the lowest common denominator of two essentially different systems. Thus, according to Soviet Chairman Khrushchev, "only such decisions should be taken in the United Nations which everyone would vote for." In more pragmatic terms, the Soviet Union has nonetheless been expanding its participation in international bodies, conventions and treaties—especially where some mutual benefit is possible. These areas include agreements on trade and on scientific and cultural exchange with Western industrialized nations and trade, aid and political agreements with developing nations. In addition, there has apparently been some "regularization" of Soviet relations with its East European satellites, particularly in the economic field. Certain aspects of trade and domestic economic policy appear to be subject to negotiation, rather than dictation by Moscow as in the past. In short, the Soviet Union is submitting larger areas of its international relations to treaty regulation—within the Soviet bloc, with underdeveloped nations, and with the West. While this may be international law at its most elementary level, it demonstrates nonetheless that the Soviet Union is sensitive to the principle of reciprocity and mutual benefit. It is still open to question whether Moscow will find it desirable to extend this same principle into political relations and enforceable arms agreements that are more comprehensive than the 1963 self-enforcing test-ban treaty. It is not at all clear that the strategy of "peaceful coexistence" will lead in any such direction. Developments within the Communist bloc, especially the Moscow-Peking ideological dispute (which also divides Communist parties throughout the world) will no doubt bear on this question.

TOWARD UNIVERSAL LAW?

To the extent that the world, in Hammarskjold's words, "is in the transition" to a larger community of law, this progress is so far mainly confined to those occasions when the *political* interests of nations and groups of nations coincide on a common rule or legal principle.

On the principle of nonaggression, for example, the Soviet bloc and the West have never been able to agree on a mutually acceptable definition. Yet, in the Suez crisis of 1956 the United States and the Soviet Union joined in condemning a specific act of aggression—the Anglo-French and Israeli invasions. However, simultaneously and in the same forum—the UN Security Council—the United States, Britain and France joined to condemn Soviet aggression in suppressing the Hungarian revolution. In both examples the position taken served the political aims as well as the traditional values of the powers concerned. (Some U. S. observers took comfort in the fact that only the United States was consistent in condemning both actions. Some British, French and Israeli observers noted that their governments, at least, bowed to UN and world pressure and withdrew from Egypt, while the Soviet Union remained in Hungary to crush the revolution.)

International law is weakest and most primitive in those areas where the political interests of nations are in deepest conflict. International law is strongest in those areas where nations have a common interest in predictable rules and procedures—especially straightforward rules that do not easily lend themselves to misinterpretation.

It is also clear that as nations grow functionally more interdependent, and as their interests increasingly overlap or conflict, the utility of clear rules and commonly accepted principles is multiplying. The "old order" is in process of change as technological and human revolutions advance and as various nations try to push the world in directions that suit their interests. A major question is what shape a "new order" may take—and whether the world will be able to avoid dangerous conflict in the transitional period.

LAW AND THE INDIVIDUAL

There is another and perhaps more fundamental problem. This is the frequent clash — domestically and internationally — between the rights or interests of the state and the rights and interests of the individual. It is a domestic legal dilemma which harasses nearly all nations, democratic or Communist, modern or modernizing. It is reflected in the problem of balancing liberty with responsibility, individual freedom with national security, pluralism and initiative with social conformity, private property with social good.

Internationally this clash of rights and interests impinges on the question of the "legal" limits of national sovereignty. In a capsule: to what extent should emerging international law concern itself with human rights, status of women, rights of private property, slavery, suppression of minority rights, self-determination of cultural minorities, religious and/or political freedom, or private responsibility for crimes against humanity? The Nuremburg war crimes trials after World War II, for example, introduced the highly controversial precedent that individuals may be tried and punished for war crimes carried out under official policies of their governments.

Normally, international law is concerned exclusively with relations among governments of nation-states. Yet there are circumstances—a UN peace-force operation, for example—when a recalcitrant individual or group of individuals may obstruct the mission of an international authority. The issue arose many times in the Congo. It could arise in a variety of ways in an expansion of international law such as an inspected test-ban treaty or general and complete disarmament.

All these questions, which are sporadically debated in international conferences, have a direct bearing on the shape of any emerging world order. They are at the heart of the problem of "sovereignty"—whether sovereignty is summed up in the absolute and unlimitable powers of a nation-state or whether sovereignty resides finally with the peoples of nations, who may delegate, if they choose, certain powers to supranational or world agencies.

PROPOSALS TO EXPAND THE RULE OF LAW

A number of thoughtful persons have reached the conclusion that peaceful change in the world will be possible in the future only if major steps are taken to expand and strengthen the rule of international law. In the midst of the Suez and Hungarian crises, in October 1956, President Eisenhower declared, "There can be no peace without law." That is, peace can be assured only if the international power system is brought under the restraint of law.

Proposals to accomplish this may be grouped loosely into three general approaches:

1. STRENGTHENED INTERNATIONAL LAW.

This approach relies on a "maturing" of the existing power system without any marked curtailment of the sovereignty of nations, except perhaps in the military field. Stability would depend fundamentally on treaty arrangements—for arms control or disarmament, peaceful settlement of disputes, trade expansion, cooperation in world development, and any other multilateral initiatives that would strike a more tolerable balance between the independence and the interdependence of nations in today's world. Codification of existing international law, by the already established International Law Commission, and perhaps with the cooperation of private legal groups such as the recently initiated World Peace Through Law Center, would contribute to this maturing process. Various nations, including the United States and the Soviet Union, might withdraw their reservations which now limit the jurisdiction of the International Court of Justice. Other steps might be taken to expand that jurisdiction still further. Hopefully, in such a changing environment, national restraints on the use of power would be strengthened, the dangers of violence would be reduced and international change could be managed more peacefully.

2. STRENGTHENED REGIONAL OR SUPRANATIONAL LAW.

This approach takes it for granted that the principal ideological, cultural, economic and other divisions in today's world will persist for some time to come. It also assumes that politics and war now operate on far too large a scale to be entrusted to the present power system of numerous sovereign and "equal" states. What is proposed, therefore, is an international power structure that is midway between the nation-state system (an obsolete system) and a single world community under universal law (an unattainable system, at least for the foreseeable future). It would be based on regional unions, federations or confederations of nations. The precedents for such structures already exist in regional groupings of nations which are interdependent economically (such

as the European Economic Community — EEC or Common Market)
or which share common problems, security interests or cultural values
(such as the OAS, the recently established Organization for African
Unity, the Atlantic Community, the Arab unity movement, the Communist bloc, etc.). Within each grouping, a body of *supranational* law
would presumably emerge, to deal with disputes within the region. The
common forum for all regional groupings would presumably be the UN.
This is where interbloc competition, disputes and conflicts would be
managed under whatever body of *international* law the politics of the
system would permit to emerge.

(In Western circles there is widespread discussion of regionalism in a
somewhat different sense — as the potential model for a new world
order based on those nations sharing Western ethical and political values.
This approach assumes that the cold war is certain to continue for the
foreseeable future but that "hot" war can probably be deterred. A corollary is that a strong, progressive and prosperous community of industrialized democracies, together with many of the developing nations, can
probably outlast the threat of Communist expansionism. That is to say,
communism may ultimately be forced to abandon its aims of a global
Communist system and may then accept peaceful competition, rather
than hostile coexistence, as the basis for international relations.)

3. VARIOUS LEVELS OF WORLD LAW.

This approach assumes that law cannot operate effectively in the
world — especially in the area of controlling international violence —
unless it is enacted, applied and enforced universally by a properly constituted world authority. World law in this sense (as distinguished from
international and supranational law) is a form of law which does not
now exist. The UN, as you have seen, does not now have such powers.
World law could come into being if a world government were set up,
either by agreement among the world's sovereign nations or in the aftermath of World War III and the victory of one nation or bloc of nations
— the United States and its allies, the Communist bloc, or a group of
other nations left relatively intact after a catclysmic great-power conflict. Or world law could come into being by universal agreement, in
certain limited areas of international relations, such as the control of
force, the resolution of international disputes and the enforcement of

disarmament and peace. The Clark-Sohn proposals deal with world law in this more restricted sense.

LOOKING AHEAD

It is a question of considerable importance — to all nations and peoples — whether international law can become a more effective instrument for the peaceful management of international relations in a rapidly changing world. Any new treaty — a trade pact, a nuclear test ban, a copyright agreement, or a nonaggression pact — represents an effort to extend somewhat the rule of law. It is an exchange of commitments to a legal principle or a set of rules. Both treaty law and customary international law are still limited in scope and lack universal acceptance. The body of international law cannot expand coherently without reconciling or overcoming competing political outlooks as well as divergent legal philosophies. Yet the question remains, Are there grounds of mutual interest — reciprocity — on which competing nations can build a better set of rules to monitor their necessary contacts with each other?

SUGGESTED READINGS:

MENDLOVITZ, pp. 77-187.

United Nations Charter, Articles 1 and 2, and Chapters IV, V, VI, VII, and VIII (Articles 9-54).

ADDITIONAL READINGS:

CALVOCORESSI, PETER. *World Order and New States.* London: Chatto and Windus for the Institute of Strategic Studies, 1962.

LISSITZYN, OLIVER J. "International Law in a Divided World." *International Conciliation.* No. 542: 1-69 (March, 1963).

TUNKIN, GREGORY I. "Coexistence and International Law." *Recueil des Cours,* No. 3: 1-81, 1958.

YALEM, RONALD. "Regionalism and World Order." *Int. Org.* 16: 460-471, (Oct. 1962).

REFERENCES:

BORGESE, G. A. *Foundations of the World Republic.* Chicago: University of Chicago Press, 1953.

HOFFMAN, STANLEY. "International Systems and International Law." *World Politics.* 14: 205-237, (Oct. 1961).

LAPENNA, IVO. "International Law Viewed Through Soviet Eyes." *Yearbook of World Affairs:* 204-232, 1961.

McDOUGAL, MYERS S. AND FLORENTINO F. FELICIANO. *Law and Minimum World Public Order; The Legal Regulation of International Coercion.* New Haven: Yale University Press, 1961.

DE VISSCHER, CHARLES. *Theory and Reality in Public International Law.* Translated from the French by P. E. Corbett. Princeton, New Jersey: Princeton University Press, 1957.

WRIGHT, QUINCY. *The Role of International Law in the Elimination of War.* NY: Oceana, 1961.

Session One   QUESTIONS FOR REFLECTION OR DISCUSSION

1. What is international law?

It is sometimes said that there is no such thing as "international law." How would you evaluate, refute or defend such a proposition? If there is no international law, how do nations conduct ordinary political and commercial relations? If there is international law, how does it function and to what extent does it regulate or influence national behavior?

What factors, other than international law, influence and restrain national governments in their relationships with other governments? What factors tend to restrain governments in their use of force in international relations? What role does international law play (if any) in limiting the use of force?

2. Do nations observe international law?

What kinds of international agreements and commitments do nations normally observe? Under what circumstances is a major power likely to "violate" international law or operate "outside" generally accepted rules of international law? Under what circumstances is a lesser power likely to do the same?

What pressures now exist in the world community (if any) to discourage breaches of international law or deviations from accepted rules of international conduct? Are any of these pressures being strengthened now? Could they be strengthened more? How?

3. *Can law help control or prevent international violence?*

How effective is the UN Charter provision, pledging all member nations to "refrain . . . from the threat or use of force"? Under what conditions might such a pledge be more effective?

Under what form would law be most effective in helping to prevent war — some strengthening of present international law, some systems of supranational law based on well defined regional groupings, or some form of world law?

Is war the responsibility of impersonal governments, or individual persons, or both? Can law effectively regulate violence and prevent war if it is applicable only to governments?

SUMMARY QUESTION:

Are there clear limits to the effective application and enforcement of international law in the contemporary world power system? If so, what are they?

ENFORCING PEACE—WHETHER IN CITY STREETS
or on the borders of two hostile nations—implies the use of *legalized*
force to prevent or suppress the outbreak of *illegal* or *unauthorized*
violence. It implies, in other words, an armed police force backed by
some form of recognized law.

At the local level, the arms may consist of night sticks, revolvers,
tear gas, riot guns or fire hoses. The law behind local police action may
be local ordinances, state or Federal statutes, or Constitutional law expressed in a court order.

In international conflicts the applicable law may be a treaty such
as the UN Charter, or a peace-enforcement resolution of a UN body
acting under the Charter. UN arms may consist of light infantry weapons in the hands of token units or a fully armed land-sea-air striking
force. An effective peace force, local or international, requires both the
moral force of law and adequate physical force to carry out its specific
mission. It also requires continuing clear guidance, by responsible authorities operating under law, throughout the duration of the mission.

In the two previous sessions you discussed various ways in which
violence can break out in an international system based on competitive
national power, and you examined the present state of international law,
especially as it relates to the threat or use of force. In this session you
will analyze efforts by the UN to enforce peace in several recent crisis
situations. On the basis of this analysis you will evaluate alternative
proposals for strengthening or improving the capacity of the world community to enforce peace under law.

INTERNATIONAL POLICE ACTION

In earlier centuries, police action in international affairs was nothing more than an extension of each sovereign nation's right to defend
its own territory against external threats, protect such interests as ship-

ping and the person and property of its nationals residing abroad, and guarantee the security of its colonies, economic and political dependencies, or allies. Major powers such as Great Britain undertook special international police functions—such as eradication of piracy and slave trade on the high seas—in the interests of the international community and as an expression of national moral concern. The Roosevelt Corollary to the Monroe Doctrine, announced in 1904 and repudiated by Washington in the 1930's, appropriated to the United States an international police power to maintain domestic order, under certain circumstances, within Latin American countries.

International police action did not receive formal, broadly based status in international law, however, until the Treaty of Versailles (1919), which established the League of Nations. The Covenant of the League defined various peace-enforcement pressures ranging from moral authority, through economic sanctions, to armed intervention in case of aggression. League members were to contribute, when asked, from their regular military forces for this purpose. In practice, armed intervention was never employed and lesser measures frequently proved inadequate.

The framers of the UN Charter envisaged an international police force that would be put together from national military units held in readiness, on a stand-by basis, by member nations. The Security Council, which under the Charter is charged with "primary responsibilitiy" for the maintenance of peace, would call up the force to maintain or restore peace when all measures short of force had failed. Under Chapter VII of the Charter the Council was authorized to order military "demonstrations, blockade, and other operations by air, sea or land forces" (Article 42) and to negotiate agreements with member nations concerning "the numbers and types of forces" that each nation would earmark, "their degree of readiness and general location, and the nature of the facilities and assistance to be provided" by each nation. These agreements were to be negotiated "as soon as possible" (Article 43).

In addition, a Military Staff Committee was established "to advise and assist" the Council in the use of the peace force. The committee consists of the chiefs-of-staff (or their representatives) of the five permanent members of the Council — that is, the nations with right of veto (Article 47). Whether a specific police action would employ military units from all member states, or from selected states, was to be determined by the Council (Article 48).

The agreements on stand-by national military units have never been negotiated. The Military Staff Committee has been virtually unused. Make-up of each of the eight UN peace missions between 1945 and 1963, was determined at the time and usually by the Secretary-General rather than by the Security Council. In short, Chapter VII of the Charter is inoperative in these key provisions covering the establishment of a stand-by UN police power on call to the Security Council.

AUTHORIZING UN POLICE ACTION

The largest UN peace-enforcement operation to date was the 1950-53 Korean police action, which assumed the proportions of a major conventional war. Military units from sixteen member nations were recruited by the Security Council without reference to Article 43. The Council authorized the action, unhampered by veto, during a temporary Soviet boycott of the Council. (The Soviet Union had walked out on the issue of seating Communist China.)

In November 1950 the General Assembly passed the Uniting for Peace Resolution, which provided for emergency action by the General Assembly in the event a veto prevented the Security Council from acting in any future crisis. In case of deadlock in the 11-nation Security Council, any seven members of the Council were authorized to vote to convene an emergency session of the Assembly. The resolution also called on member nations to maintain stand-by military units "that could be promptly made available" to either the Security Council or General Assembly, without any of the formal agreements called for in Article 43.

This special stand-by provision has yet to be carried out, although in April 1963 Denmark, Norway and Sweden agreed among themselves to set up a 3,000-man international "fire brigade" which could be placed at the disposal of either the Security Council or the General Assembly in an emergency.

The main effect of the Uniting for Peace Resolution has been to divide the UN's peace-enforcement responsibility between the Security Council and the General Assembly, a situation which the Soviet Union and France consider illegal. (Even so, in both the 1956 Suez and 1958

Lebanese crises the Soviet Union favored invoking the Uniting for Peace Resolution to call emergency sessions of the General Assembly.)

When the Council was unable to act in the Suez crisis of 1956 (because of British and French vetoes), the General Assembly set up the UN Emergency Force (UNEF). In the 1958 crisis in Lebanon the Security Council reached veto-free agreement to send a UN observer group to help prevent illegal infiltration of arms and personnel into Lebanon. In 1960 the Security Council authorized a UN peace force for the Congo (ONUC, after the French initials designating the force) but policy direction over the Congo operation rotated between the Council and the Assembly. In 1963 the Security Council, after prolonged behind-the-scenes negotiations, authorized a small UN observer force to oversee the disengagement of United Arab Republic and Saudi Arabian military forces from opposing sides in the civil war in Yemen.

Each of these police actions has raised constitutional and political questions about authorizing, recruiting, directing and financing UN peace forces. Equally important questions have risen about the effectiveness of these operations — whether they have had adequate physical, as well as legal, force to carry out their missions, and whether they have received adequate guidance from the responsible UN organs. The complexity of these problems will be apparent in a review of two distinctive police actions: UNEF and ONUC.

UNEF: A DEMONSTRATION FORCE

The Suez crisis of October-November 1956 directly involved two major powers, Britain and France, along with Israel, in military action against Egyptian (now U.A.R.) troops and territory. (The Anglo-French invasion was billed as a police action, to "separate" the Israeli and Egyptian fighting forces and secure the recently nationalized Suez Canal in the interests of maritime trade.) The two superpowers were indirectly involved because of the potential explosiveness of the situation — the Soviet Union, in the name of anti-imperialism and as a supporter of President Gamal Abdel Nasser of Egypt; the United States, as an opponent of military aggression in spite of its NATO alliance with two of the invading powers.

Britain and France expressed willingness to turn over their "police" function to the UN, provided there was a return to the *status quo ante,* including steps toward denationalization of the Canal. No such solution could have survived a Soviet veto in the Security Council, nor were the United States and other Council members amenable to this approach. Two cease-fire resolutions were vetoed by Britain and France. On a Yugoslav motion, the crisis moved to an emergency session of the General Assembly, where a sequence of resolutions called for an immediate cease-fire, withdrawal of invading forces and reopening of the Canal. Secretary General Hammarskjold was asked to submit, within 48 hours, a plan for UN peace-force intervention. The plan was prepared, calling for a force made up of units from smaller nations, and was approved in the Assembly by a vote of 57-0 with 19 abstentions.

In spite of the explosive controversies which had created the crisis, the political situation was favorable for an effective "demonstration" or token UN police action, rather than a fighting force. The invading powers were already committed to withdraw in favor of the UN and kept their pledge (although with some foot-dragging) as UNEF moved in. Whatever its misgivings about the failure to "punish the aggressors," the Soviet bloc elected to abstain rather than vote against the Assembly resolution. Perhaps most important, both Egypt and Israel — the two hostile powers whose borders were to come under UN surveillance — agreed in advance to the purposes and make-up of the UNEF operation.

FUNCTIONS AND LIMITATIONS OF UNEF

UNEF (which has never numbered much more than 6,000 men) is really a token-force border patrol. It is lightly armed and overwhelmingly outnumbered on both sides. It was sent in, not to restore or maintain order by means of force, but to verify symbolically that order *had been* restored and to provide hostage that Egypt and Israel would honor their pledges (within bounds) not to break the peace. Behind UNEF were a substantial majority of the UN and a favorable world opinion. The chief armament of UNEF was and is local recognition of, and deference to, the moral force of the UN itself. It may also be assumed that the United Arab Republic and Israel have preferred a UN-supervised truce to open war.

No permanent peace has been established, however, on U.A.R.-Israeli borders. Seven years later UNEF remained at its desert posts. Despite mediation efforts, there has been no negotiation on border or refugee disputes. Political tensions and the U.A.R.-Israeli arms race continue (as do small-scale border raids, in spite of UNEF), and technically the state of hostilities continues, as it has since 1948. To this extent, the UN peace-enforcement effort in the Middle East has failed — it polices a truce; it has not restored or constructed a basis for peace. (And, because UNEF was set up by the General Assembly, rather than by the Security Council, and was planned, recruited and directed by the Secretary-General, rather than under the provisions of Article 43, it has raised constitutional questions of "legality" and has contributed to the UN financial crisis — a matter you will pursue in the next session.)

ONUC: A FIGHTING FORCE

The UN peace-force operation in the Congo, ONUC, faced from the beginning very different conditions and obstacles than UNEF, and raised more serious legal and political problems within the UN. To a much greater degree than in the Middle East, the Congo crisis of 1960 raised the spectre of a direct superpower confrontation. Unlike the Suez crisis, where the United States and the Soviet Union were more or less "on the same side," the Congo found both superpowers at odds — and various lesser powers, including the African states and several U.S. NATO allies, at odds with each other, with various Congo factions and with the UN. As events developed, it became clear that a major function of ONUC was to try to prevent the Congo from becoming a cold war battleground.

Belgium granted independence to the Congo on June 30, 1960 on unexpectedly short notice, and with little advance preparation. Within days the new nation had fallen into chaos—army mutiny, secessionist moves in several provinces, bloody intertribal clashes, and pillaging and violence against, primarily, the European population.

As white administrators, technicians and civilians fled the country, Belgium rushed in fresh troops in an uninvited effort to restore order and protect its extensive mining and other interests. However, this military move violated the independence treaty. Moreover, in Katanga province, which produces 60 per cent of the country's wealth, Belgians apparently encouraged local authorities who favored secession from the central government.

The Congo central government asked the United States for military aid, but Washington, anxious to avoid a big-power confrontation, suggested a multilateral approach. The Congo then appealed to the UN, "not to restore the internal situation in Congo but rather to protect the national territory against acts of aggression committed by Belgian metropolitan troops."

The Secretary-General (acting for the first time under powers provided in Article 99) convened the Security Council. After an all-night debate, the Security Council (with Britain, China and France abstaining) adopted a vague and ambiguous resolution. It called on Belgium to withdraw its troops and authorized the Secretary-General, in consultation with the Congo government, "to provide . . . such military assistance as may be necessary until, through the efforts of the Congolese Government with the technical assistance of the United Nations, the national security forces may be able, in the opinion of the [Congo] Government, to meet fully their tasks."

All details were left to the Secretary-General, including the composition and operational control of the peace force. Hammarskjold set the following broad terms (confirmed in a later Security Council resolution):

1. ONUC would be recruited primarily from African nations and a few other small powers; it would include no forces from the great powers nor from any nation with interests in the Congo.

2. ONUC would avoid involvement in the Congo's internal conflicts, would have freedom of movement and would not take the initiative in using force — it would "act only in self-defense."

ONUC MOVES IN

Within eight days of the Congo's appeal, the UN had one Irish, one Swedish and twelve African battalions in the Congo. The twenty-one (mostly African) nations which ultimately furnished troops formed an Advisory Committee to Hammarskjold, performing both political and military staff functions.

As ONUC moved in, some Belgian forces moved out but a significant number of Belgian officers and advisers, and Belgian and other foreign mercenaries, remained in Katanga province, where they reinforced the secessionist aims of provincial president Moise Tshombe. Despite negotiations, promises and token moves, the secession problem in Katanga and other provinces continued to plague the UN (and the Congo central government) until early 1963.

In addition, a power struggle developed within the central Congo government soon after ONUC moved in. Key figure in the struggle was Premier Patrice Lumumba, whose immediate objectives were to force the evacuation of all remaining Belgian and mercenary troops and to integrate the secessionist provinces into a strongly centralized national government — by force if necessary. Other factions in the Congo government, including President Joseph Kasavubu, opposed Lumumba's design for centralization although they by no means favored dismemberment of the country. The UN was caught in the political crossfire.

Lumumba looked to ONUC to help him achieve his objectives. ONUC, however, had no authority to interfere in the internal political conflicts of the Congo, including the question of whether the Congo should become a unitary state or a confederation of states. Moreover, ONUC was not authorized by the Security Council to use force, except in self-defense.

In the Security Council, the Soviet Union and Poland demanded that ONUC shoot its way into Katanga. Hammarskjold insisted that ONUC could not do so unless the Council specifically so instructed it. Any such resolution had little likelihood of adoption and none was introduced. (Nations contributing forces to ONUC had been assured of the self-defense principle.) In its third resolution on the Congo the Council instead reaffirmed the principles that had guided Hammarskjold: Belgian troops must withdraw and ONUC must enter Katanga, but the UN "will not be a party to or in any way intervene in or be used to influence the outcome of any internal conflict, constitutional or otherwise." Armed with this resolution, Hammarskjold secured Tshombe's cooperation in admitting a token ONUC force, which the Secretary-General personally led into Katanga province in mid-August 1960.

COLD WAR SHOWDOWN

Lumumba was wholly dissatisfied with Hammarskjold's noninterventionist approach. He turned to friendly nations for aid — especially Ghana, Guinea, the United Arab Republic and the Soviet Union. Ghana and Guinea threatened to withdraw their military units from ONUC and place them at Lumumba's disposal for a military conquest of Katanga. By the end of August, Soviet, Czech and other military equipment was pouring into the Congo. In secessionist South Kasai province, Lumumba launched a campaign which degenerated into civilian massacres ("genocide," Hammarskjold later called it).

At one point, direct Soviet military intervention on Lumumba's behalf seemed such a real possibility that the United States informed the Security Council it was prepared to join with other UN nations to "do whatever may be necessary to prevent the intrusion of military forces not requested by the UN."

In mid-September 1960 an effort was made in the Security Council to clarify the UN's role in the Congo and to make explicit what was already implied — that the UN should be the sole channel for military forces and supplies entering the Congo. The Soviet Union vetoed the declaration. The General Assembly then took up the matter in emergency session and voted 70-0 authorizing the Secretary-General to continue assisting the central government "in the restoration and maintenance of law and order throughout the territory of the Republic of the Congo and to safeguard its unity, territorial integrity and political independence." The Assembly also appealed to all member nations to "refrain from the direct and indirect provision of arms" independent of the UN operation and called for "speedy solution by peaceful means of all . . . internal conflicts." (The Soviet Union, France, South Africa and some 30 other powers abstained.)

This action did not represent a change of heart on the part of Lumumba's African allies who voted for the resolution; it did represent the only alternative to an outright repudiation of Hammarskjold and ONUC. It also appeared to be the only way to keep the great powers — and the cold war — out of the Congo, a goal which the United States and most African countries shared with Hammarskjold.

CHANGE OF MISSION

Meanwhile, a moderate military faction seized control of the central government, detained Lumumba and ordered all Soviet personnel out of the Congo. After a brief period under UN protection, Lumumba escaped, was captured by Congolese forces, sent to Katanga and, apparently, murdered. But the country remained divided and on the brink of civil war.

In late 1960 the Soviet Union introduced a resolution in the Security Council calling for a complete withdrawal of the UN, especially its armed forces, from the Congo. The resolution received no support and a substitute resolution was passed which authorized ONUC to "take immediately all appropriate measures to prevent the occurrence of civil war in the Congo, including . . . the use of force, if necessary, in the last resort." Provision was also made for reconvening the Congo parliament, for bringing Congo military units under discipline and control, and to evacuate all foreign military personnel, including political advisers.

As the UN became more deeply involved in the internal affairs of the Congo (and as Soviet and other unilateral intervention was cut off) Hammarskjold came under sharper attack from Moscow. As early as the fall of 1960, in fact, Chairman Khrushchev was demanding the Secretary-General's resignation or dismissal and the creation of a three-man *"troika"* executive for the UN. The Soviet campaign continued until Hammarskjold's death in September 1961 (while on a mission to Katanga).

African powers which had joined the Soviet Union in opposition to ONUC, and which also had intervened unilaterally in Congo affairs, made peace with the Secretary-General by the fall of 1960. When they had to choose between supporting a UN operation they did not like and converting the Congo into a cold war battleground, they chose the UN. They also joined with the majority of the UN membership to reject *troika.*

The essence of ONUC's difficulties in the Congo was that the Secretary-General (first Hammarskjold and later Thant) had to act in a succession of crises even though neither the Security Council nor the General Assembly could agree on what action, or power of discretion, he should be authorized to employ. If the member nations of the Organization could not agree to provide ONUC with clear policy guidance, then, in Hammarskjold's words, they ought to accept either the actions that were taken or "the responsibility for inaction." As it happened, they preferred to accept neither.

Not until late 1962 did the Soviet Union give even tacit support to ONUC. The occasion was Secretary General Thant's decision to make a show of force in Katanga in order to pressure Tshombe into keeping his agreements with the central government. The alternative appeared to be a reopening of civil war. The decision had open backing from the United States and tacit approval of the Soviet Union, although it was opposed by Britain and France. The issue was not voted on in the Security Council. The show of force was made. Tshombe's military resistance collapsed and a political settlement of the Katanga secession was achieved some months later. The UN's role in these developments is still a subject of controversy.

LESSONS OF UNEF AND ONUC

The experiences of UNEF and ONUC reveal a number of weaknesses, both technical and political, of past practices in UN peace-enforcement. The principal *technical* weaknesses are the following:

1. ADEQUATE FORCE.

Since UNEF has performed as a demonstration force, rather than a fighting force, the size of the operation has not been important. ONUC, however, found itself inadequate and outnumbered in various clashes with mutinous Congo troops, hostile civilian mobs and secessionist Katanga troops. Although it was part of its primary mission to maintain law and order, ONUC lacked sufficient physical power to do so until late in the operation, by which time the Congo central government and army had achieved some stability and discipline. The problem could be much more serious in some future police action in which the UN faced determined and prolonged military resistance.

2. PHYSICAL CONTINUITY.

Some nations contributing forces to UNEF withdrew them because they felt they could not afford such a long-term diversion of crack troops. This might have jeopardized UNEF's mission had it not been for the willingness of other nations to provide substitute troops. ONUC's mission *was* jeopardized when several nations withdrew troops (or threatened to do so) in deliberate efforts to influence or frustrate the Secretary-General's policy. The UN cannot carry out a police action if it cannot count on the availability of adequate forces for the duration of the mission.

3. FINANCIAL CONTINUITY.

Both UNEF and ONUC have been of longer duration and greater cost than originally anticipated. The effectiveness of both police actions has been imperiled by the controversy over finances — a problem you will explore in the next session.

UNEF and ONUC also revealed serious *political* weaknesses in the present system, including the following problems:

1. PRIMARY RESPONSIBILITY.

Conflicts among the great and lesser powers, especially among the five veto-wielding permanent members of the Security Council, have tended to divide peace-enforcement responsibilities, not only between the Security Council and General Assembly, but also with the Secretary-General. The absence of decisive political control over peace forces raises legal questions as well as problems of practicality. The Soviet Union and France, for example, consider past UN peace-force operations illegal because they were not set up and conducted in strict accordance with the letter of the Charter.

2. CLEAR-CUT MANDATE.

One of the most serious problems arising from diffused responsibility and loose political control is the difficulty of obtaining, under these conditions, a precise definition of the peace force's mission. Should it use force, other than in self-defense? Should it have the right to intervene in domestic affairs and, if so, under what circumstances and to what extent? Should it have the power to detain or punish recalcitrant individuals? ONUC was plagued with these problems, particularly the question of intervention. Various Congo factions, including Tshombe and the central government, criticized ONUC at different times for intervening or for failing to intervene. Various UN member nations criticized ONUC for operating as an invading army, rather than as an international police force, especially in the winter of 1962-63 when ONUC mounted a limited offensive against Tshombe's hold-out troops in Katanga.

3. POLITICAL NEUTRALITY.

ONUC commanders were unable to rely on a few of the national units under their control, some of which favored Lumumba and his political heirs. In addition, factions in the Congo attempted to utilize ONUC forces for their own political aims. Finally, authorized ONUC policy — however neutral in intent — occasionally favored one local faction over another. For example, when UN officials silenced the radio and seized the airports in the capital in an effort to prevent the outbreak of civil war, the effect was to cut Lumumba off from the rest of the country and weaken him politically.

4. PEACE-BUILDING MACHINERY.

As mentioned earlier, UNEF has had to remain on duty for seven years because neither the UN nor any other body has been able to resolve the fundamental political conflict between the United Arab Republic and Israel. The UN has been somewhat more successful in the Congo, where its technical assistance program — supplemented by direct assistance to the Congo from other nations, such as Belgium, Nigeria and the United States — has helped restore reasonable civil order. An important element in the new stability was the reintegration of Katanga and other secessionist areas into the republic, partly as a result of UN military and political pressure on Tshombe. Some observers are disturbed, however, that unification of the Congo involved the UN in the use of force to influence the outcome of an "internal" dispute.

Obviously, the technical and political problems of effective peace-enforcement are closely related. Most of the technical difficulties would disappear if UN members (especially the great powers) reached political agreement on the whole peace-enforcement system. A standardized procedure, acceptable to all, would eliminate the need for hastily recruited *ad hoc* forces. It would also eliminate the diffusion of responsibility and the other weaknesses which hamper the effectiveness of these emergency operations.

LETTER VERSUS SPIRIT OF THE CHARTER

One alternative to the present system is to carry out the letter of Chapter VII of the Charter. This is the Soviet position, which France shares. If the agreements under Article 43 were negotiated, many of the current problems would vanish. The UN would be assured of adequate physical force for most situations because it could call up as many stand-by military units as it needed, and could retain control over these units as long as necessary—if the Security Council gave the required political authorization. Financial continuity would presumably be assured by prior agreement in the Security Council. Primary responsibility for maintaining peace would be restored to the Security Council and the line of command, through the Military Staff Committee, would relieve the Secretary-General of his present controversial responsibilities. Nations sitting on the Security Council would be unable to escape responsibility for their own inaction, or for their failure to agree on action.

There would also be certain dangers. The negotiated agreements under Article 43 would, in effect, give the Security Council *exclusive* power to call up a UN peace force made up of the stand-by units held in readiness by member governments. Thus the Council would have exclusive initiative for peace-enforcement. One veto on the Council would be enough to prevent any UN action in a specific crisis. The letter of the Charter would be observed but the spirit and intent of the Charter—"To maintain international peace and security"—would be in danger of violation.

For this basic reason the United States, Britain and a substantial number of other UN members opposed carrying out the provisions of Chapter VII. They share the view that the UN must have the power to act even against the wishes of any one of the five great powers, and that measures to make this possible (such as the Uniting for Peace Resolution) are wholly legal implementations of the intent of the Charter.

OTHER PEACE-FORCE ALTERNATIVES

There are other alternatives. There is ample latitude under the Charter for various kinds of stand-by or permanent peace forces to be established, provided agreement could be reached on a formula.

The Secretary-General, for example, could recruit a permanent volunteer peace force as part of the Secretariat staff. He would need nothing more than budgetary approval from the General Assembly to establish the force although only the Security Council or General Assembly could order the force into action. At a less ambitious level, the Secretary-General could issue UN military training manuals or could even train a corps of officers from those countries likely to provide UN forces in an emergency. He might also set up an expanded military staff unit at UN headquarters. (Secretary General Thant recently appointed a permanent military adviser.)

Or the Security Council could recruit a stand-by or permanent UN force made up of volunteers or of military units from member countries, without invoking the full provisions of Chapter VII. This would require great-power unanimity, however.

Or the General Assembly, under its powers of recommendation, could specify the make-up of a permanent or stand-by peace force, could approve a budget to finance it, and could then "recommend" to member nations that they contribute personnel or complete military units to it.

Or UN member nations, acting individually, could earmark specially trained military units for UN service, available on call to either the Security Council or General Assembly. As noted earlier, three Scandinavian countries have already taken this step, first envisaged in the 1950 Uniting for Peace Resolution.

Finally, it is theoretically possible to take a giant step by creating a permanent UN peace force that would be large enough to take over from individual nations exclusive responsibility for international security. It will be useful to examine the Clark-Sohn proposals for such a force, bearing in mind that this would be part of a total plan based on universal disarmament and the world legislative and executive proposals you have already noted in earlier sessions.

PEACE-ENFORCEMENT IN A DISARMED WORLD

A fundamental hypothesis underlying the total Clark-Sohn plan is that effective peace-enforcement is impossible so long as major national military forces remain in existence. An essential step, therefore, is universal and complete disarmament of national military forces under a world law prohibiting rearmament and the threat or use of force between nations.

Yet war would still be possible, although on a far more primitive scale. In a disarmed world there would still be local police forces equipped with small arms and, conceivably, with riot guns and enough light artillery to put down civil rebellions. Private citizens would no doubt have access to sporting arms. Presumably, therefore, a nation with a strong grievance or outsize ambition could mobilize substantial firepower for an attack on another nation that was (at the most) no better armed. Finally, the technology of rearmament (including the manufacture of nuclear weapons) would be suspended, not forgotten, with the advent of disarmament. If the grievances between nations were grave enough, a disarmed world could rapidly rearm.

The Clark-Sohn plan, in other words, is a disarmament-enforcement as well as a peace-enforcement plan. Essentially it proposes a set of inter-related measures to reduce the dangers of, the opportunities for and the causes behind major international violence. Even then, the experts admit that international violence may occur—but at manageable levels that are short of holocaust.

Clark and Sohn propose, that even in a disarmed world an effective peace-enforcement blueprint should have some such characteristics as the following:

1. ADEQUATE MILITARY FORCE.

The plan calls for 200,000 to 300,000 men in a standing professional military force plus a stand-by reserve of from 600,000 to 1.2 million. The standing force would be stationed around the world, at UN bases. The deployment arrangement would insure (a) no undue concentration of troops in any one area, (b) no UN troops in the twelve largest nations, and (c) ready UN access to any crisis situation that might develop. Units would be highly mobile and would control their own transport. They would be armed with the latest weapons — including nuclear weapons, in reserve, in case one nation brought a nuclear arsenal out of hiding in the midst of a crisis. (Initially the UN would acquire its armaments from demobilized national stockpiles; later it would manufacture its own arms.)

2. CLEAR-CUT MANDATE.

The chain of command for the peace force would begin with a Military Staff Committee made up of five professional military commanders recruited from the smaller powers. This military staff would be under civilian control of the Executive Council (the Clark-Sohn name for a reconstituted Security Council). The Executive Council (minus veto) would function as agent of the General Assembly, which, in turn, would have primary responsibility for defining the mission of any peace-keeping operation, as well as the responsibility for financing it. The General Assembly, in other words, would have ultimate responsibilty for providing — or failing to provide — a clear-cut mandate to any peace-force operation.

3. POLITICAL NEUTRALITY.

Members of the standing force and the stand-by reserve would all be individually recruited volunteers. Furthermore, recruitment would be primarily from the small nations. No single nation would be allowed to supply enlistments which added up to more than 3 percent of the entire UN force, or of any branch of the force, or of the officer corps. The professional allegiance of peace-force volunteers would belong to the UN, rather than to any single government.

4. PHYSICAL CONTINUITY.

Because of the recruiting policy described in the previous paragraph, there would be no possibility that a nation could suddenly withdraw whole units it had loaned to the UN.

5. FINANCIAL CONTINUITY.

The Clark-Sohn plan also calls for adequate and reliable revenue arrangements (which you will examine in detail in the next session.)

6. PEACE-BUILDING MACHINERY.

Finally, the plan lays great emphasis on a judicial and conciliation system and on greatly expanded efforts to speed world economic development. The authors consider these measures essential if some of the causes leading to war are to be uprooted. They attach particular importance to the judicial and conciliation system since it would provide peaceful procedures for settling legal and political disputes which otherwise might be resolved by force.

A JUDICIAL AND CONCILIATION SYSTEM
UNDER WORLD LAW

In the Clark-Sohn plan, the judicial and conciliation system would be equipped to deal not only with justiciable legal problems (such as disputes over the meaning of treaties) but also with complex political problems (such as border disputes, refugee problems and such delicate issues as the Katanga secession) which may endanger the peace. It would be, in essence, a world judicial, quasijudicial and conciliation system designed to settle all international disputes by peaceful means and to uphold and administer laws against the international use of force. It would include the following elements:

1. INTERNATIONAL COURT OF JUSTICE.

The Court's jurisdiction would be greatly expanded and clearly defined in all areas related to disarmament, peace-enforcement and the compulsory resolution of disputes which threaten the peace. The General Assembly would have the power to *direct* member nations to submit such disputes to the Court and the Court's decision would be binding and enforceable, by UN military power if necessary.

2. WORLD EQUITY TRIBUNAL.

Normally this body would make recommendations on disputes not subject to adjudication according to recognized legal principles in international law. However, in cases where these recommendations received special support (say a three-fourths vote) in the General Assembly on a peace-threat issue, then the recommendations would be mandatory and enforceable.

3. UN REGIONAL COURTS.

Some twenty to forty of these would be established around the world to try *individual* violators of the world law prohibiting rearmament and the threat or use of force between nations.

Individuals serving in this world judicial and conciliation system would be appointed for life by the General Assembly under various precautionary safeguards. Thus the world judiciary would be "internationalized" in the service of the world community as represented by the UN.

LOOKING AHEAD

The heart of the problem is whether it is possible, in the present international system, to enforce peace under the restraint of law. This is a dual question. It concerns the adequacy of present legal processes —as well as the adequacy of physical arrangements—for meeting threats to the peace and for restoring or maintaining order. If the answer is negative, then the problem is to determine what steps the world community can or should take to insure that international competition, conflict and change will be nonviolent and equitable for the nations and peoples involved.

SUGGESTED READINGS:

MENDLOVITZ pp. 304-352.

CLARK AND SOHN, pp. xxix-xxxv; 89-128, 175-182, 314-344.

ADDITIONAL READINGS:

CLAUDE, INIS L., JR. "United Nations Use of Force." *Conflict Resolution* 7: 117-129 (June, 1963).

GROSS, LEO. "Some Observations on the International Court of Justice." *American Journal of International Law* 56: 33-62 (Jan 1962).

LARSON, ARTHUR. *Questions and Answers on the World Court.* Durham, N. C.: World Rule of Law Center, Duke University Law School, 1960.

MILLER, E. M. "Legal Aspects of U. N. Action in the Congo." *American Journal of International Law* 55: 1-28 (Jan. 1961).

MUNRO, SIR LESLIE. "Can the United Nations Enforce Peace?" *Foreign Affairs* 38: 209-218 (Jan. 1960).

REFERENCES:

BLOOMFIELD, LINCOLN P. "International Force—A Symposium." *Int. Org.* 17: 321-485 (Spring, 1963).

GORDON, KING. *The United Nations in the Congo.* NY: Carnegie Endowment, 1962.

LARSON, ARTHUR. *When Nations Disagree; A Handbook on Peace Through Law.* Baton Rouge: Louisiana State University Press, 1961.

STONE, JULIUS. *Legal Controls of International Conflict; A Treatise on the Dynamics of Disputes and War Law.* NY: Rhinehart, 1954; with supplement: London: Stevens, 1959.

SEYERSTED, FINN. "United Nations Forces: Some Legal Problems." *British Yearbook Intl. L.* 37: 351-475 (1961).

Session Three   QUESTIONS FOR REFLECTION OR DISCUSSION

1. What is peace-enforcement?

What are the purposes of international peace-keeping? Are there any important differences between the concept of a "police force" and the concept of an "army"? In this respect, were there significant differences in the way UNEF and ONUC operated? If so, what were they? Did UN forces in Korea operate as a police force or as an army?

What useful purposes has UNEF performed? What are its limitations or weaknesses? In balance, do you feel it has been accomplishing its mission?

What useful purposes did ONUC perform? What were its limitations or weaknesses? In balance, did it accomplish its mission?

2. What are the conditions which make effective peace-enforcement possible?

The Suez and Hungarian crises broke at the same time. UNEF was mobilized and sent into the Middle East. Why was there no similar UN intervention in Hungary?

In your opinion, why is there no international peace force operation in the disputed border areas between India and Communist China? in Berlin?

What conditions must be present before a UN peace-force operation can be established?

3. What are some possible alternatives to past peace-force operations?

In your opinion, what are likely to be the most important advantages and disadvantages of each of the following alternative ways of organizing a UN peace force?

a. Recruiting an *ad hoc* force, with the cooperation of member nations, whenever it is needed (present system).

b. Stand-by national military units, on call to the Security Council, as provided in the inoperative articles of Chapter VII of the Charter.

c. A permanent, standing peace force that is always under arms and is deployed under permanent UN command.

d. Any of the other alternatives suggested on pages 55-56.

Which of these alternatives (or combinations of alternatives) would be most effective in your opinion? If you favor a permanent standing force, would you also feel it should be made up of individual volunteers, as suggested by Clark and Sohn? Why or why not?

Do you think effective peace-enforcement is possible without universal disarmament? Why or why not?

SUMMARY QUESTION:

What safeguards are desirable or essential to insure that a peace-enforcement operation is conducted according to fair, just and equitable principles? What kind of political control over the peace force would serve these ends? Is an effective judicial and conciliation system also desirable or essential? Why or why not?

GRAVE FINANCIAL CRISIS PURSUED THE UN through 1961-62 and into the middle of 1963, threatening the two major peace-enforcement operations, UNEF and ONUC, with bankruptcy. Emergency measures initiated by the General Assembly in the regular sessions of 1961 and 1962, and in a resumed session in June 1963, staved off collapse of the peace forces, at least until the end of 1963. The fundamental causes of the financial crisis were not removed, however; they were simply made temporarily manageable.

Yet, as a result of the ordeal, the UN emerged in several respects stronger. Issues were clarified. Some of the inequities in the revenue and assessment system were aired and partially rectified or at least compromised. Substantial majorities of the membership adopted several principles to guide the financing of future peace-enforcement operations. Finally, those nations that had refused to pay past peace-force assessments (and had thus aggravated the financial problem) were urged to distinguish between the solvency of the Organization and any political or juridical reservations they might have about past assessment methods.

In this session you will examine the causes and magnitude of the UN's financing problems, steps taken so far to deal with these problems, challenges that remain to be resolved, and alternative proposals for more reliable and adequate revenue systems.

ORIGINS OF THE FINANCIAL CRISIS

At the beginning of 1962 the UN faced a deficit of $111.7 million —the gap between total liabilities and cash on hand. The deficit climbed to $149 million in mid-1962 but tapered off to around $100 million a year later, largely as a result of the sale of specially authorized UN bonds and voluntary contributions. There have been three principal causes of this persistent deficit:

1. Increased demand for aid and services to members, combined with a growing membership. (Membership has more than doubled since the UN was founded in 1945; the assessed or regular budget has increased by 60 percent since the mid-1950's—from $50 million to $82 million a year.)
2. Establishment of two costly peace-enforcement operations: UNEF in 1956 and ONUC in 1960. (Combined cost of these two operations has been running about $140 million a year.)
3. Inability of some members to pay their assessed shares of the rising costs and the refusal of others to share in the costs of UNEF and ONUC.

The situation has political and juridical implications, as well as serious financial consequences. During the first ten years of the Organization, member states were assessed only for the regular UN budget and the administrative budgets of the specialized agencies. All other funds—over half of all UN expenses—were raised through voluntary contributions.

Beginning with UNEF, however, the General Assembly introduced the practice of assessing the costs of peace-force operations on the same scale as the assessments for the regular budget. Thus, especially after the establishment of ONUC, the UN became increasingly dependent on assessments—binding obligations on all members—rather than on voluntary contributions. In 1963 the budget breakdown was as follows: *assessments* (regular budget, administrative budgets of specialized agencies and UNEF and ONUC) totaled over $300 million; *voluntary contributions* added up to about $150 million.

This new practice created special hardships for the poorer nations, many of whose annual assessments were increased by more than 40 per cent. In addition, a number of nations objected to the new system on political grounds—that all or a major share of the peace-enforcement costs should be borne by the "aggressors," or by the permanent members of the Security Council, or by the industrialized and wealthy nations. Some nations objected on constitutional grounds—that the General Assembly has no authority under the Charter to dictate financial arrangements for peace-enforcement operations since the Security Council, under Chapter VII, has "primary responsibility" in this field.

As of mid-1963, 24 nations had expressed their inability to pay—or had refused to pay—any part of their assessed share of UNEF's cost and 46 nations had paid nothing toward the costs of ONUC. The UN's total cash deficit at that time was roughly equal to the total arrears for these two peace-force operations.

PROBLEM OF ABILITY TO PAY

By far the simplest problem to deal with is the claimed inability of some of the poorer nations to pay UNEF and ONUC assessments on top of their obligations toward the regular UN budget.

The regular budget is currently running at a little over $82 million a year. Two-thirds of this is assessed to the five permanent members of the Security Council on the following scale (1962-64): United States, 32.02 percent; Britain, 7.58 percent; China (Republic of China), 4.57 percent; France, 5.94 percent; Soviet Union, 14.97 percent (17.47 percent if Byelorussia and the Ukraine are included, both integral parts of the Soviet Union but with separate votes in the General Assembly). The U.S. assessment toward the regular budget in 1961 amounted to $22,332,800. In 1961 the smallest assessed share of the regular budget was 0.04 percent, or $27,478. A total of 29 nations were assessed this minimum amount.

The costs of UNEF were running close to $1.6 million a month during 1960-62 and were budgeted at $1.58 million a month for the first six months of 1963. The costs of ONUC ran around $10 million a month during 1962 and were so budgeted for the first six months of 1963. The 29 poorer nations, at the 0.04 percent rate, would thus be assessed $3,700 for UNEF and $7,900 for ONUC. Added to the assessment for the regular budget this meant a total UN assessment of $39,078.

Acting on the assumption that this was too great a hardship for the poorer nations, the General Assembly voted in the fall of 1960 to reduce somewhat the peace-force assessments for those Latin American and newly admitted states already in arrears or in danger of becoming so. The resulting deficits were made up by voluntary contributions from other nations, chiefly the United States.

This step eased but did not fully resolve the problem of many of the poorer nations. As of mid-1963, $6 million was past due on the

1962 regular budget (half from the Republic of China, the balance from other nations with internal financial difficulties). Another $500,000 was past due on the 1961 regular budget (mostly from Latin American states). Only Haiti was in arrears for 1959-60. Further steps (which you will examine later) were taken on this problem by succeeding General Assembly sessions.

PROBLEM OF REFUSAL TO PAY

The political and juridical aspects of the financing crisis have been far more difficult to deal with. They stem from the manner in which UNEF and ONUC have been financed, and from varying interpretations of the UN Charter and the separation of powers between the General Assembly and the Security Council.

When British and French vetoes prevented the Security Council from acting in the Suez crisis of 1956, the General Assembly voted to establish UNEF to patrol the Egyptian-Israeli border and supervise the truce. The Assembly also voted that the costs of this peace-force operation would be assessed to the full membership on the same scale as the regular budget. The decision was bitterly opposed by the Soviet Union and the Arab states, which argued that the full costs of UNEF should be borne by the "aggressor" states—Britain, France and Israel. Furthermore, the Soviet Union challenged the General Assembly's authority to specify the financing arrangements for a peace-enforcement operation.

In 1960 the Security Council authorized an even more ambitious peace-force undertaking for the Congo—ONUC—but made no provisions for financing it. The General Assembly, in spite of the UNEF experience, voted to finance ONUC according to the regular budget scale of assessments. The Soviet Union, several African and Middle Eastern states, France and Belgium protested the decision, some of them for different reasons. (To the Soviet Union, Belgium and the United States were the aggressors in the Congo and should foot the bill for ONUC; to some of the African and Arab states, Belgium should have borne the whole cost; to France and Belgium, the financial arrangements could legally be made only by the Security Council—a view which the Soviet Union also shared.)

The constitutional or juridical question is whether the General

Assembly has the authority to control the financing of peace-enforcement operations. Since this authority is denied by France and the Soviet Union, whose combined share adds up to over 20 percent of the total costs of UNEF and ONUC, and since several other nations have also withheld their assessments because of unwillingness or inability to pay, the practical financial consequences have been serious. As of June 30, 1963 France and the Soviet Union and the Republic of China were responsible for $70 million of the total $100 million in arrears on the two peace-keeping accounts.

In addition, the constitutional stand—that only the Security Council is competent to control the financing of peace-force operations—is related to the political stand of some other nations that feel the members of the Security Council, especially the four permanent members that are industrialized, should bear the major burden. This position is based on the premises that these nations have the largest responsibility for maintaining world peace and, at the same time, the greatest economic capacity for financing the effort.

ATTEMPTS TO RESOLVE THE FINANCIAL CRISIS

A special Working Group was established by the Fifteenth General Assembly (convened in September 1960) to study and make recommendations on this complex of problems. With modifications and enlargements, the committee was continued by succeeding Assemblies.

Meanwhile, faced with the immediate threat of insolvency, the Sixteenth General Assembly (fall of 1961) took two important initiatives:

1. UN BOND ISSUE.

As an urgent, stop-gap measure the General Assembly authorized (by a vote of 58 for, 13 against and 24 abstentions) the issuance of $200 million in UN bonds at 2 percent interest. Principal and interest are to be repaid from the regular budget in twenty-five annual installments. The bond issue, however, "should not be deemed a precedent for the future financing of" UN expenses.

The step is important, not only because it enabled the UN to acquire needed cash and thus avoid—or at least postpone—insolvency, but also because it had the effect of distributing as much as $200 million worth of UNEF and ONUC expenses among the entire membership. That is, by providing for repayment of the loan and servicing costs *from the regular budget,* the General Assembly made this much of the "extraordinary" expenses of the Organization into "ordinary" expenses —assessable to all members. (This precedent, however, was later challenged by France and the Soviet Union.)

The U.S. Congress authorized the purchase of up to 50 percent of the entire bond issue on a matching basis. Later Assembly sessions extended the deadline for negotiating the sale of the bonds, first to June 30, 1963 and then to December 31, 1963. By mid-1963 purchases and pledges, including U.S. matching purchases, were near $140 million, sufficient to cover the July 1, 1962–June 30, 1963 costs of the two peace-keeping operations.

(In a related action, the Sixteenth Assembly increased the UN's revolving capital fund from $25 million to $40 million, further strengthening the Organization's cash position.)

2. INTERNATIONAL COURT ADVISORY OPINION.

The Sixteenth General Assembly also resolved to ask the International Court of Justice for an advisory opinion on the legal question whether the Assembly had the right to apportion UNEF and ONUC expenses among the full membership. After hearing arguments from all sides, including Russian arguments that this was a political, not a legal, question and therefore was not within the competence of the Court, the Court issued a 9-5 opinion on July 20, 1962.

In its opinion, the Court affirmed its competence to take up the issue as "an essentially judicial task, namely, the interpretation of a treaty [i.e., UN Charter] provision." The Court then advised that the action of the General Assembly had been legal under Article 17, paragraph 2, which provides that "the expenses of the Organization shall be borne by the Members as apportioned by the General Assembly." In the Court's opinion the word "expenses" means "all the expenses and not just certain types of expenses." The Court considered it irrelevant whether the peace forces were established by the Security Council or the General Assembly. As long as a UN organ established the forces, the expenses are a legal obligation of the Organization and were within the competence of the Assembly to assess.

The Court did not advise (it had not been asked) how the expenses should be apportioned or assessed; this is a matter for the General Assembly to decide under powers granted by the Charter. Thus the scale of assessments could be the same or different from that used in apportioning the regular budget. Or, if the General Assembly had so voted, the expenses for UNEF and ONUC could have been apportioned to the "aggressor states," as the Soviet Union and some other nations wished. The choice of alternatives is up to the General Assembly in each case.

By "accepting" the Court's advisory opinion (in a 76-17 vote in December 1962) the General Assembly, in effect, made it obligatory for all members—including France and the Soviet Union—to pay their assessed shares of the two peace-force budgets as well as the regular budget. Even so, France and the Soviet Union continued to insist that the peace-force assessments were illegal and the Court's opinion had no legal effect.

OBLIGATION AND PENALTY

It is important to recognize that the General Assembly's power to apportion the expenses of the Organization, as defined in Article 17, paragraph 2, is the only power granted by the Charter to the Assembly which is legally binding on all member states. Indeed, Article 19 provides a penalty for failure to fulfill this obligation:

> "A Member of the United Nations which is in arrears in the payment of its financial contributions to the Organization shall have no vote in the General Assembly if the amount of its arrears equals or exceeds the amount of the contributions due from it for the preceding two full years. . . ."

This penalty is not automatic, however. Article 19 concludes: "The General Assembly may, nevertheless, permit such a Member to vote if it is satisfied that the failure to pay is due to conditions beyond the control of the Member."

The first near-test of this Charter provision came in May 1963 when Haiti's arrears exceeded the two-year limit at the point that the resumed General Assembly session on finances was convened. The question was raised in the corridors whether the penalty—suspension of Haiti's vote—would be invoked automatically by the President of the Assembly, Muhammad Zafrulla Khan of Pakistan, or whether a vote of the full membership would be requested. A number of delegations, including the United States, were anxious to have the penalty invoked automatically in order to establish a precedent that would be applicable to the Soviet Union in January 1964, unless it pays $9 million in arrears before then, and to France probably sometime in 1965.

As it turned out, the Haitian delegation absented itself from the General Assembly during the early days of the meeting and no issues came up for vote during its absence. Haiti soon presented a check large enough to absolve it from the penalty. In a letter to the chairman of the Assembly's Fifth (budgetary) Committee, Kahn indicated, however, that he would have announced the suspension of Haiti's vote automatically, without calling for a decision by the membership, had the payment not been made. No question was raised concerning that provision in the Charter under which Haiti might still have retained its vote had the Assembly satisfied itself that failure to pay was "due to conditions beyond the control of the Member."

Although no clear precedent was established in this case, the Soviet Union went on record insisting that the suspension of a member-state's voting rights is an "important question" within the meaning of Article 18, paragraph 2, and that it would therefore require a two-thirds majority of the members present and voting. This paragraph includes "the suspension of the rights and privileges of membership" and "the expulsion of members" among a list of "important questions."

This controversy may not come to a real test until either the Soviet Union or France is two years in arrears in its financial obligations to the Organization. (As permanent members of the Security Council, both would retain their vote in the Council even if they lost it in the Assembly.)

FURTHER EFFORTS TO DEAL WITH FINANCES

In accepting the Court's advisory opinion, the 1962 General Assembly also took official cognizance of the complaints of the poorer nations. It passed a resolution recognizing that some nations are in no position to contribute to the UN's extraordinary expenses on the same scale as their assessments for the regular budget.

The Working Group set up to study all aspects of the financing problem was asked to bear this problem in mind. In addition, the group was called on "to study . . . special methods for financing peace-keeping operations . . . involving heavy expenditures such as those for the Congo and the Middle East, including a possible scale of assessments. . . ." The Working Group was to examine the "special responsibility of the Security Council," the specific character of a peace-keeping operation which might have a bearing on how costs should be shared (who was the victim and who was the aggressor), and "the degree of economic development of each Member State and whether or not a developing State is in receipt of technical assistance from the United Nations." Finally, the Working Group was to make recommendations to the Assembly on how the problems of arrears, and penalties, on peace-keeping assessments should be handled.

The group was instructed to submit its recommendations to a resumed session of the Assembly, scheduled for May–June 1963. The group met in the spring of 1963, under chairmanship of the Nigerian ambassador to the UN, but failed to produce a report.

RESUMED GENERAL ASSEMBLY SESSION

The General Assembly reconvened May 14 and, after exhaustive debate in committee, and considerable corridor diplomacy, passed seven resolutions on financing. Briefly, the resolutions accomplished the following:

1. and 2. The two resolutions of greatest urgency authorized the Secretary-General to spend the $42.5 million necessary to finance UNEF ($9.5 million) and ONUC ($33 million) for the last six months of 1963. Costs for the period July 1, 1962 through June 30, 1963 were to be covered by proceeds from the sale of UN bonds. Thus the two peace-force operations gained a six-month lease on life. ONUC's military operations would be phased out by the end of 1963 and any further technical assistance to the Congo would be financed by voluntary contributions. The refinancing of UNEF into 1964 was left to

the Eighteenth General Assembly to resolve in the fall of 1963. In addition, the two resolutions provided for a scaling down of the peace-force assessments of the poorer nations and classified all but the twenty-six most advanced nations in the poorer category. The precise formula provided that the first $2.5 million for UNEF and the first $3 million for ONUC would be raised according to the scale of assessments for the regular budget. Thereafter the poorer nations would pay only 45 percent of the regular scale. The resulting $3.7 million deficit was assigned to the advanced nations in the form of voluntary contributions. The United States pledged nearly $2 million for this purpose.

3. A resolution on general principles to govern the financing of future peace-force operations affirmed the "collective responsibility" of the full membership. Within this collective responsibility, however, note was taken of the special responsibility of the advanced countries and particularly the five permanent members of the Security Council (even though one of the permanent members, the Republic of China, was classified as one of the eighty-five poorer nations in the previous resolutions). The resolution also called for "special consideration," when warranted, of the financial responsibility of "victims" in a breach of the peace as opposed to the responsibility of nations "otherwise involved"—a euphemism for aggressors. This provision was inserted at the insistence of the Arab states.

4. Those nations responsible for the $100 million in arrears were urged to pay up in order to preserve the solvency of the UN, but without necessarily acknowledging any legal obligations in setting up the peace forces in the first place and without prejudice to any political or juridical reservations they still had regarding the method of financing.

5. The deadline for the sale of UN bonds was extended till the end of 1963.

6. The Assembly authorized a study of the feasibility of a "peace fund" which would be permitted to accept donations from in-

dividuals and organizations as well as from governments. The purpose would be to create a reserve fund that would allow the UN to act quickly in a crisis without waiting for approval of a financing plan.

7. The twenty-one-nation Working Group was authorized to continue until 1964 its study of a new scale of assessments for peace-keeping operations.

UNRESOLVED PROBLEMS

This intricate set of resolutions only partially softened the financial crisis. The $42.5 million peace-force assessment for the second half of 1963 will produce only about $28 million if France, the Soviet Union and other reluctant nations continue to withhold payment. The UN's peace-force deficit at the end of 1963 may amount to $120 million on peace-force assessments, plus the 25-year indebtedness on $140 million or more in bonds.

There were other loose threads which the General Assembly session on finances failed to tie, including two unresolved problems of paramount importance. One was the juridical dispute over the power of the General Assembly to apportion *all* expenses of the organization, including the costs of peace-keeping, or any part of them it chose, according to a scale of assessments binding on all members. This authority was clearly asserted by a substantial majority of the Assembly and had been supported by the advisory opinion of the International Court but it continued to be strongly contested by two permanent members of the Security Council.

The second paramount question was political—whether the membership could and would enforce the penalty under Article 19 in the event France and the Soviet Union continued to defy the majority on the assessment issue. How to do it would be part of the problem—whether by ruling of the President of the Assembly, by simple majority vote of the full membership, or by two-thirds vote. Whether even to attempt invoking the penalty against a permanent member of the Security Council, moreover, would involve political judgment of the utmost delicacy.

Yet the dilemma extends beyond just the peace-force financing issue. In January 1963 France announced it had no intention of paying its assessed share (5.94 percent) of the $4.5 million item in the *regular* budget for servicing the interest payments on the UN bond issue for the year 1963. It disapproved of the bond program, considered that the General Assembly had no authority to assess the costs of the program as a binding obligation on all members, and therefore refused to pay.

In June 1963 the Soviet Union listed five items in the regular budget which it considered illegal and therefore would not participate in financing. These were the UN bond servicing costs, the costs of the UN Commission for the Unification and Rehabilitation of Korea, maintenance of the UN cemetery in South Korea, the UN Truce Supervision Organization in Palestine, and the UN field service which supplies interpreters and other personnel for UN missions overseas. Russia's share of these costs (at 14.97 percent) added up to a deduction of well over $1.1 million.

The showdown issue, in short, was whether the General Assembly had *any* authority, under Article 17, paragraph 2, to bind all members to financing plans adopted by a majority but objected to by individual nations. France said No; only the Security Council—where the veto obtains—has authority under the Charter to compel or bind member nations. The Soviet Union concurred.

SECURITY COUNCIL INITIATIVE

While the financing debate was under way in the resumed session of the General Assembly in June 1963, the civil war in Yemen created what might have developed into a test case of the Security Council's ability to recapture the initiative in controlling peace-force finances.

The conflict was between Yemeni royalists who had been ousted in a coup some months before and Yemeni republicans who had established a provisional government that gained recognition from a number of nations, including the United States and the Soviet Union. The royalists continued to resist, with military assistance from Saudi Arabia; the republicans obtained military support from the United Arab Republic. The indecisive war reached the point where outside mediation was possible. Retired U.S. diplomat Ellsworth Bunker, acting on behalf of the UN Secretary-General, proposed a formula which was accepted by all sides: Saudi Arabia and the United Arab Republic would disengage their forces from the civil war under supervision and verification of a UN observer group.

The operation was to take no more than two months and the total costs were to be borne by the Saudi and U.A.R. governments. This was a key provision because it made it possible for the UN to carry out a peace-force operation at no cost to the UN membership-at-large, a precedent welcomed by many governments.

However, the Soviet Union insisted that the UN could not properly carry out this peace-enforcement operation unless the plan—including the financial arrangements—had been endorsed by the Security Council, the only organ competent, in Moscow's view, to authorize such an undertaking. The Soviet delegation called a session of the Security Council and urged adoption of its position as an operating element in the resolution on Yemen.

The United States and other powers on the Council refused to accept a precedent-setting resolution. After some delay and behind-scenes negotiations, the Council adopted a compromise resolution offered by Ghana and Morocco. The resolution endorsed the peace-enforcement operation but avoided mentioning finances in the operative paragraphs. The resolution was adopted 10-0, with the Soviet Union abstaining. The principle of Security Council primacy in the peace-keeping field received no new impetus.

AN UNRELIABLE REVENUE SYSTEM

Without a clear-cut resolution of the financing problem—the binding authority of General Assembly decisions on regular budget items as well as peace-enforcement costs—the entire UN revenue system suffers from unreliability. The situation might improve if the Franco-Soviet view were adopted, and binding authority were limited to the Security Council, but only on the condition that the Security Council proved itself able to reach agreement on financing—as well as establishing—a UN peace force in a crisis situation. So far, the Council has sometimes failed to agree on the nature of UN intervention in a peace threat and has yet to agree on how it should be financed, with the sole exception of Yemen. (The UN group which supervised the transition of West

Irian (West New Guinea) from Dutch to Indonesian control was also paid for by the nations involved, but the financing formula was not brought before the Security Council for ratification.)

Or the situation might improve if the General Assembly's binding authority were accepted on the basis, say, of a two-thirds vote on extraordinary expenses such as peace-enforcement. Once again, however, the reliability of such a formula would depend on whether the Assembly could reach rapid agreement on both the need to intervene and the manner of financing the intervention.

QUESTION OF PRIORITIES

The horns of the dilemma, in short, are on the one hand the urgency and adequacy of force with which the UN must move into certain crisis situations—such as the Congo—and, on the other hand, the administrative details—however burdensome—of financing the continuing operation. To date the UN has put higher priority on the first consideration. If the two considerations are to have equal priority, and must be resolved simultaneously by vote on a single resolution, then a crisis might well get out of hand long before the UN authorized itself to act. (The Yemeni crisis hung fire over a month after Saudi, U.A.R. and Yemeni agreement to the plan had been obtained—until Security Council action.)

Hypothetically, for example, a serious threat to the peace might erupt in either of Portugal's major African colonies, Angola or Mozambique, or in South or Southwest Africa. In any of these cases, other African nations, other European nations, the Soviet Union and the United States would all have vital stakes and conflicting interests. In anticipation of the event it is very difficult to imagine the Security Council reaching quick agreement on the nature, scope and financing of a UN effort to restore peace. And, if a two-thirds majority of the General Assembly were required for the same ends, this would be almost as difficult to imagine.

The priority question, in other words, is the UN's physical, financial and political ability to act quickly and with adequate force when the peace is threatened.

The problem is how much effective peace-keeping authority the sovereign members of the UN are willing to delegate to a collective agency, free of veto. The hesitancy is primarily on the part of nations who insist on right of veto when money or force is involved.

FINANCING THE UN SYSTEM

Peace-keeping, however, is only part of the UN's job. Peace-building is another, less publicized part—in the area of technical assistance, work of the specialized agencies and programs of the Economic and Social Council, Trusteeship Council, World Bank and other world development efforts. Here, too, there are important questions whether present financing systems are either reliable or adquate.

Financing of the whole UN system now falls into two broad categories:

1. *Assessments,* which include the regular budget ($82 million for 1963), the administrative budgets of the specialized agencies (about $90 million) and the two peace-keeping operations, UNEF and ONUC (combined, roughly $140 million).

2. *Voluntary* contributions (around $150 million). This category includes the UN Children's Fund (UNICEF), the Expanded Program of Technical Assistance (EPTA), the UN Special Fund, the voluntary funds administered by the UN High Commissioner for Refugees (UNHCR), etc.

These two categories together finance a total UN system that costs well under $500 million a year. (This does not include subscriber-financed UN operations such as the World Bank.)

Voluntary contributions also play a small but significant role in the financing of assessed expenses. The United States, for example, has been contributing to the support of UNEF and ONUC to make up for scaled-down assessments to some of the poorer nations, especially those receiving UN technical assistance. Until mid-1963 the United States was paying about 47.5 percent of peace-force costs. Under the new formulas this burden will be scaled down to about 37 percent. It is obviously not a long-term solution to the over-all financing problem, however, to make basic UN operations dependent on the generosity of the United States or any other government. If the scale of assessments is impractical, it presumably should be revised.

Nor would there be any clear value in converting the programs which are now voluntarily financed to an assessment-support formula. The whole principle behind these programs is that capital-exporting nations can and should bear the major costs of assisting capital-poor nations. Furthermore, a membership assessment system might discourage the important contributions of some nonmember states, such as Switzerland, West Germany and the Holy See.

There has been some pressure — especially from the Soviet Union, but also from Britain and others — to scale down the costs of various UN activities. Russia, for example, has proposed a $50 million ceiling on the regular budget. It appears unlikely, however, that the General Assembly will begin curtailing services and operations which a majority of member nations would clearly like to see expanded. In politically realistic terms, the challenge appears to be, rather, How can the UN develop a fair and reliable formula for the apportioning of expenses which are almost certain to rise rather than fall or level off?

PROSPECTS FOR REFORM

A number of reforms of the present system are under consideration.

The cash position of the UN has been improved by the increase in the revolving or Working Capital Fund (from $25 million to $40 million). This position would be improved still further if member nations would pay their assessments in regular installments — perhaps monthly — instead of irregularly (and frequently late) as is the current practice. The Swedish delegate suggested some time ago that the UN should charge interest on outstanding contributions to encourage prompter remittances. Establishment of a stand-by peace fund, as proposed by the 1963 resumed session of the Assembly, could help.

Some progress has already been made (as you noted earlier) in working out a fairer scale of assessments covering UNEF and ONUC and it may become possible to spell out the financing formula for any future peace-force operation as an integral part of the original authorizing resolution. (It is also possible that this would make it even more difficult to get agreement on a Security Council or General Assembly resolution in a crisis situation where immediate action was required.)

There is even the possibility that the Soviet Union, France and other reluctant nations will ultimately accept as ineluctable the International Court's advisory opinion and will become current in their past-due accounts.

Reforms, improved efficiency and fuller cooperation from all members would remove some of the irritants, inequities and uncertainties from the present revenue system. Certain other problems would remain.

The question of *adequate* revenues for the UN does not appear close to solution in the current tug and haul over UN spending. Some important contributors seem determined to pare or at least hold down expenses while most of the new nations are demanding expanded Secretariat services and higher outlays for technical assistance to health, education, resource development and other growth needs. Cold war politics, the high cost of the arms race and wide divergences in political and economic aims help postpone any real solution to this problem, even though the wide gap between rich and poor nations is, in itself, a source of international tension.

The question of *reliability* of UN revenues may also escape solution unless there is a major overhaul either in the revenue system or in the attitudes and commitments of member nations. There is nothing in the present system to force a member nation to pay its assessment for a program it opposes for political or juridicial reasons. By refusing to pay, it risks losing its vote in the General Assembly but even if this penalty is invoked, that will not provide the UN with the revenues that have been withheld. There is even some question whether it will be politically feasible or desirable to invoke the penalty specified in Article 19, especially against a major power.

A NONPOLITICAL REVENUE SYSTEM?

The most radical overhaul suggested so far is the Clark-Sohn proposal to remove UN financing from the political arena by creating a world-wide, tax-based revenue system which would be written into world law as an annex to the UN Charter. Out of the savings from disarmament (the foundation of the Clark-Sohn plan), the system would substantially increase UN revenues in an effort to insure *adequate* investment in world economic and social development. By making the system an integral part of the Charter, the authors of the plan also hope to insure its *reliability*.

The main feature of the plan is that the UN would be assigned, in advance, all or part of certain taxes which each nation would designate and assess under its own national laws. The UN, in other words, would enjoy the benefits of predictable revenue from a global tax system — but without the burden or costs of having to collect the taxes. Tax-collection would continue to be a national responsibility.

Even the procedure for legislating the annual UN budget would become less political. Under the present system the entire UN membership sitting as a committee of the whole (Fifth Committee) develops the budget on the basis of the Secretary-General's proposals and the comments of an advisory committee. Under the Clark-Sohn proposal, a standing committee of the General Assembly — a much smaller body, presumably including budget specialists — would develop the budget on the basis of proposals submitted by staff. In both systems, of course, budgetary approval could be granted only by a plenary session of the General Assembly.

The greatly strengthened UN which Clark and Sohn envisage would be a far more expensive system than the present $500 million-a-year UN. It would also be set up to accomplish much more. It would have the authority and the manpower to enforce peace in a disarmed world. The standing UN peace force which you discussed in the previous session (and which would be the only military force in the world) would cost about $9 billion a year—about 7½ percent of current annual military expenditures of all nations. The expanded UN would also include a new World Development Authority with an annual budget of perhaps $25 billion — roughly one-quarter of the total U.S. aid program (loans and grants, economic and military) from the end of World War II until mid-1963. Finally, the anticipated expansion of Secretariat, specialized agency and other functions of a strengthened UN would cost, according to Clark and Sohn, about $2 billion a year. So, in the round, the Clark-Sohn "peace system" would cost about $36 billion a year — 72 times as much as the present UN, two-fifths of the U.S. national budget for the fiscal year 1964, and one-third of what the world has been spending annually on armaments.

IMPLICATIONS OF BINDING FINANCIAL OBLIGATIONS

An immediate question, however, is how the present UN can be put on a fair, adequate and reliable financial base — with or without important structural reforms. The main feature of the Clark-Sohn revenue proposal is that it would institutionalize UN financing. The total revenue plan would be worked out in advance; politics would intervene only in the process of budgeting expenditures. The main characteristic of the present system is that UN financing may be in *transition* in this same direction. This is one implication of the controversy over UNEF and ONUC assessments. By accepting the International Court's advisory opinion, the General Assembly has rejected the principle that any nation may exercise a "financial veto" by refusing to pay its share of any of the Organization's expenses which the General Assembly votes to apportion among the whole membership.

If the UN is indeed moving in this direction — if the General Assembly's power to enact binding financial obligations on all members is universally accepted — then the Organization may be taking a small but important step toward effective peace-enforcement based on a reliable revenue system. The only power of enforcement now available under the Charter is the power to deny a vote to any nation more than two years in arrears (Article 19). Yet the penalty is an important one, a test case may not be far off, and it is conceivable that a substantial majority of the UN membership may be in a mood to invoke it.

At stake is the same principle with which Clark and Sohn are concerned: the capacity of the Organization to legislate to the extent necessary to carry out its primary mission of maintaining international peace and security. Adequate and reliable revenues are essential to this mission.

There is a possible future impasse in that the General Assembly might assert the power to budget and assess a considerably expanded world economic and social development program. The burden of such a program would fall chiefly on the richer nations, and especially the United States. But, under its current foreign policy, the United States channels the vast bulk of its foreign aid through bilateral and regional arrangements, rather than through the UN. The UN is viewed from Washington as well as from Paris, London and Moscow, as *an* instrument of diplomacy, not as *the* central force or over-all framework in world politics. The advanced nations may find common cause in discouraging any broad evolution of the General Assembly's financing powers.

LOOKING AHEAD

The recent (and as yet unabated) financial crisis in the UN has forced some important issues to the fore. They may be summed up briefly as a continuing search for politically acceptable formulas which will insure fairly apportioned, adequate and reliable revenues to finance the UN system. Past practices have proved themselves inadequate. Major changes — in principle and practice — are already in process or under serious consideration. The resolution of these issues will involve political and legal as well as financial considerations. The immediate question is what direction the UN membership should take now, and what political action on finances will best serve the long-term interests of the UN and the world community.

SUGGESTED READINGS:

MENDLOVITZ, pp. 355-358.

United Nations Charter, Articles 17 and 19.

CLARK AND SOHN, pp. xxxvi-xxxix, 132-136, 345-348.

ADDITIONAL READINGS:

"Assembly Accepts Court's Opinion on Peace-Keeping Expenses." *UN Review* 10: 46-55, (Jan. 1963).

HOGG, JAMES F. "Peace-Keeping Costs and Charter Obligations — Implications on the International Court of Justice Decision on Certain Expenses of the United Nations." *Columbia Law Review* 62: 1230-1263, (Nov. 1962).

ROSENSTEIN-RODAN, P. N. "International Aid for Underdeveloped Countries." *R. Economic Statistics* 43: 107-138, (May, 1961).

SCHMIDT, WILSON E. "Development Aid and Disarmament." *Disarmament and the Economy,* edited by Emile Benoit and Kenneth E. Boulding. NY: Harper and Row, 1963.

REFERENCES:

GROSS, LEO. "Expenses of the UN for Peace-Keeping Operations: The Advisory Opinion of the International Court of Justice." *Int. Org.* 17: 1-35, (Winter, 1963).

INTERNATIONAL COURT OF JUSTICE. "Certain Expenses of the United Nations." Advisory Opinion of July 20, 1962. *I. C. J. Reports:* 151-368, 1962.

JACKSON, JOHN H. "The Legal Framework of United Nations Financing: Peacekeeping and Penury." *California L. R.* 51: 79-133, (March, 1963).

JACKSON, COMMANDER SIR ROBERT. "An International Development Authority." *Foreign Affairs* 37: 54-68, (Oct. 1958).

SINGER, JOEL D. Financing International Organization; *The UN Budget Process.* The Hague: Nijhoff, 1961.

Session Four   **QUESTIONS FOR REFLECTION OR DISCUSSION**

1. Are present UN finances adequate?

Looking at the total UN budget (page 77), do you feel it is adequate, too high or too low? Should some UN functions — administrative, peace-keeping, voluntarily financed technical assistance programs — be expanded or reduced? Why or why not?

Should there be greater emphasis on voluntary financing? Or on assessments binding on the full membership? Do you feel the scale of assessments for the regular budget, which assigns two-thirds of the total cost to the five permanent members, is fair or unfair? Why or why not?

2. Are present UN financing systems reliable?

Review the seven financing resolutions passed by the Assembly in June 1963 (pages 71–73). What does each of these resolutions accomplish — and fail to accomplish?

Is the UN on a sounder financial basis as a result of these resolutions? What uncertainties still remain?

Presume France and the Soviet Union continue to withhold payment on peace-force and regular budget items to which they object. When either country becomes two years in arrears in its payments, should the General Assembly invoke Article 19 in order to suspend French and Soviet voting privileges in the General Assembly? Why or why not? What are some of the possible consequences of invoking this rule? of not invoking it?

3. *What are the alternatives to the present financing system?*

Apart from voluntary contributions from governments and private sources, a number of other revenue alternatives have been suggested. Do you think any of the following alternatives would be desirable or feasible?

    a. A UN revenue stamp on all mail crossing international boundaries.

    b. A UN revenue tax on airplanes crossing international boundaries.

    c. UN tolls on international waterways.

    d. Assigning to the UN ownership of minerals in Antarctica, ocean beds and/or outer space.

    e. Interest charges on outstanding assessments owed the UN.

SUMMARY QUESTION:

What are the advantages and disadvantages — especially in terms of adequacy and reliability — of the global taxing system recommended by Clark and Sohn?

CONTROVERSIES OVER THE SETTING UP OF PEACE
forces and over the power of the General Assembly to enact binding
financial obligations on UN members are, in the final analysis, constitutional issues. The underlying question in each case may be expressed
in two parts:

1. In entering into the elaborate treaty commitments contained in
   the UN Charter, how much authority (apart from the peace-
   keeping authority) have member nations irreversibly delegated
   to the international organization?

2. To what extent does the Organization itself, as a legal political
   entity, have the power to act collectively to enforce its decisions
   on reluctant members?

This is a constitutional question in the sense that any written compact among sovereign states — the UN Charter, the Treaty of Rome
which set up the Common Market, or the Articles of Confederation
which first brought the thirteen American colonies into a political union
— usually spells out certain powers delegated to the union and reserves
other powers to the member states. Some functions and powers of the
union may simply by implied in general terms. Furthermore, as conditions change within such a union, the members may consent to a constitutional evolution. They may agree that the *intent* of the treaty,
charter or constitution calls for some enlargement or curtailment of the
powers of the union, or for a stricter or looser interpretation of the
written compact. A compact may even provide for a judicial board or
body to rule on interpretational disputes.

In relation to UN organs, however, the International Court appears
to have only an "advisory" function on legal questions (Article 96 of

the Charter). Thus the Court's advisory opinion on the General Assembly's assessment powers was, as noted in the previous session, "accepted" by vote of the Assembly. In a sense, therefore, disputes over the interpretation of the Charter are political rather than legal — subject to political debate and vote rather than final judicial decision. Individual nations, like France and the Soviet Union, may continue to dissent from what they believe to be "illegal" UN actions, even after the Court has expressed an opinion and the majority view has been expressed in an Assembly vote. To the extent that the dissenting nations are able successfully to defy the majority, the result is a constitutional deadlock.

In such a situation the majority may act collectively to enforce its view — by invoking Article 19 on the finance question, for example. Yet, even though it may establish the precedent, it still has no power to enforce its will on the reluctant members (or even to collect the controversial assessments). The members may continue to sit in the Assembly without voting or paying. If the members walk out, then the UN itself is weakened numerically, financially and in its power to influence international relations. It becomes less universal and its jurisdiction is significantly cut back. Indeed, the League of Nations receded into oblivion via this route.

EFFECTIVE WORLD AUTHORITY

The problem is an acute one for the UN, whose fundamental purposes are universal. That is to say, the determination of "the peoples of the United Nations . . . to save succeeding generations from the scourge of war" (Preamble) cannot be carried out effectively in only part, even a major part, of the world; it is a goal that can be realized only on a global basis. Similarly, the determination "to establish conditions under which justice and respect for the obligations arising from treaties and other sources of international law can be maintained" (Preamble) applies to international law throughout the world, not merely in parts of it. Finally, the pledge "to unite our strength to maintain international peace and security" (Preamble) implies that the Organization, as a collective entity, has been delegated certain legal jurisdictions necessary to carry out its purposes.

In this session you will explore in some detail the problem of uni-

versality in UN membership and the related problem of legal UN jurisdiction within the international system. These questions are crucial, not
only to current controversial operations of the UN, but also to the long-
term role of the UN as an effective world authority for the maintenance
of peace and security.

PROBLEM OF UNIVERSALITY

However universal the declared *purposes* of the UN, the principle
of *universality of membership* is not explicit in the Charter nor was it
uppermost in the minds of the Charter-framers. The "original members"
of the UN were those nations which were allied victoriously in World
War II against the Axis powers. Article 4 of the Charter opened membership "to all other peace-loving states which accept the obligations
contained in the present Charter and, in the judgment of the Organization, are able and willing to carry out these obligations."

In fact, the following nations were excluded from UN membership
for various political reasons until 1955: Albania, Austria, Bulgaria, Cey-
lon, Finland, Hungary, Ireland, Italy, Jordan, Libya, Nepal, Portugal,
Rumania and Spain. Japan was not admitted until 1956 and Outer
Mongolia, until 1961.

Throughout the Charter the language and procedure imply qualifications for membership and, therefore, that some nations may be excluded. Nonetheless, the Charter assigns the UN responsibility to insure
that nonmember states will "act in accordance" with the Organization's
principles "so far as may be necessary for the maintenance of international peace and security" (Article 2, paragraph 6).

Article 4 provides that new members are elected by the General
Assembly "on recommendation of the Security Council." Thus the veto
has been used to obstruct the admission of new members. (Over half
of all vetoes cast have been used to block membership applications.)
Article 5 provides, furthermore, for suspension "from the exercise of the
rights and privileges of membership" of any states against which the UN
may be engaged in preventive or enforcement action. Article 6 provides
for the expulsion of states which have "persistently violated" the principles of the Charter. During 1962-63 the Soviet Union and several
African states urged expulsion of the Republic of South Africa because

of its racial policies. Security Council action in August 1963, however, called simply for an embargo on arms shipments to South Africa and for further observation of the situation.

NONUNIVERSALITY OF THE UN

In both principle and practice, in other words, UN membership has been treated as a privilege which carries with it certain obligations. Membership is neither automatic nor universal. There are at present three categories of nonmember states:

NON-SELF-GOVERNING TERRITORIES.

That is, those areas — such as the U.S. Pacific trust territories and a few remaining colonies, protectorates and trust territories in Africa, the Middle East, Asia, Oceania and Latin America — which have not yet achieved independence and are therefore not eligible for membership.

VOLUNTARY NONMEMBERS.

Several states, for reasons of national policy, have not applied for membership. Switzerland is the largest of these. There are, in addition, the small European sovereignties of Andorra, Liechtenstein, Monaco, San Marino and Vatican City. (Some of these states, however, contribute to and are members of various UN specialized agencies and programs such as the Expanded Technical Assistance Program).

DIVIDED NATIONS.

As a result of the cold war, three nations — Germany, Korea and Vietnam — remain divided into Communist and non-Communist territories, with no immediate prospects of unification under a single government and little prospects of UN membership until unification is achieved.

In addition there is the very special case of China, which is a Charter member of the UN and one of the five permanent members of the Security Council (that is, with right of veto). China's seat in the UN has been held, since the founding of the Organization, by the government of the Republic of China although, in 1949, that government was driven from the Chinese mainland and now exercises control only over the island of Taiwan, the Penghu Islands, the islands of Quemoy and Matsu in Amoy Harbor, and a few other island outposts. The question of seating Communist representatives of the People's Republic of China (which controls the mainland) is not, therefore, a question of "admission" to the UN. It is rather a question of which Chinese government, the one on Taiwan or the one on the mainland, should occupy China's seat in the UN.

THE CHINA DEBATE

Since 1950 the question of Chinese representation has been raised regularly in the UN although until 1961 the matter was not debated in the General Assembly. Instead, as a result of parliamentary maneuver, the issue was "postponed" each year. In the Sixteenth General Assembly, which opened in September 1961, the question was admitted to debate but proposals to shift the representation to the Communist Chinese regime were decisively voted down. The issue was raised again in the Seventeenth General Assembly with the same result.

The principal arguments for seating a Communist Chinese delegation in the UN are political. The argument is sometimes based on the plea that the Communists are in effective control of virtually all of China's territory and population, that this population amounts to one-quarter of the human race, and that it is politically unrealistic to deprive these people and their goverment of a voice in UN affairs or to deprive the UN of the benefit of that voice. The argument is also often phrased in terms of universality — that the UN ought to be universal even if it is not now and that the participation of the *de facto* Chinese government is essential to this universality.

The question of disarmament lends particular urgency to both these arguments. A world disarmament program is inconceivable without full participation of Communist China as well as all other states capable of maintaining armaments and conducting war. The United States (which has led the battle to keep Communist China out of the UN) has given tacit recognition to this problem. It has been recent U.S. policy to assume that, once a disarmament agreement is reached among the principal powers other than Communist China, that country would be expected to accept the agreement and participate in the disarmament program. Communist China has said, however, that it will not consider itself bound by any agreement negotiated without its participation. Moreover, U.S. efforts to charge the Soviet Union with responsibility for insuring Communist China's compliance with any future disarmament agreement have been rebuffed by Soviet diplomats.

THE U.S. POSITION

U.S. opposition to seating a Communist delegation in the UN is, in one respect, conditional. That is to say, the United States could presumably be persuaded to withdraw its objections if Communist China were to "accept the obligations contained in the present Charter" and proved itself "able and willing to carry out these obligations" (Article 4). The United States maintains that, so far, the Communist regime has displayed open contempt for the Charter by waging war against the UN in Korea (1950-53) and by insisting on its right to use force in pursuit of national aims and in the furtherance of international Communist aims.

The crux of the U.S. position lies in a strict construction of the Charter: UN membership is a privilege which carries with it certain obligations. The United States takes the position that the Taiwan regime has accepted these obligations and is entitled to exercise the privileges of China's membership while the mainland regime is contemptuous of these obligations and is therefore not qualified to participate in the UN.

But this is only part of the U.S. position on Chinese representation. There is the equally complex political question of what to do about the Republic of China on Taiwan. Communist China has insisted on the expulsion of the Taiwan delegation from the UN and the restoration of Taiwan to mainland control. A settlement of the representation issue on Communist China's terms would, according to the U.S. view, replace a peace-loving government with a warlike government and would sacrifice 10 million Taiwanese and Chinese to Communist subjugation without any freedom of choice.

COMPROMISE PROPOSALS

This same problem has bothered other delegates at the UN, even some governments which have long mantained diplomatic relations with Communist China and which do not recognize the government of the Republic of China on Taiwan. As a result, a "two-China" solution has been proposed, giving the mainland regime China's seat in the UN, including a permanent seat on the Security Council, while retaining UN membership (that is, a seat in the General Assembly) for an independent Taiwan. Proposals have also been made for a UN-supervised plebiscite on Taiwan, after a transition period, to allow that population to decide whether it wishes to submit to mainland control, retain the present regime or establish a new government in which the Taiwanese (90 percent of the population) would have a larger voice in their own affairs than they now enjoy under the Chinese-exile regime.

Another formula would tie any shift in Chinese representation to an enlargement of the Security Council. The purpose would be to "compensate" for Communist China's acquisition of the veto by extending the same privilege to other major nations, such as India and Brazil. Additional Security Council seats (without right of veto) might also be made available to some of the newer nations which now feel they are underrepresented as a group in the 11-nation Security Council. This formula would tie the Chinese representation issue into a "package" solution that might be acceptable to more members.

Communist China and the Republic of China have both rejected any compromise in principle although the firmness of this position has not been tested in genuine negotiations. The United States, for its part, has expressed no interest in compromise either. Washington prefers to exclude Communist China from the UN until the Peking regime renounces force and in this and other ways demonstrates it is "able and willing" to carry out Charter obligations. The General Assembly votes in 1961 and 1962 indicated, in spite of the large number of abstentions, that the United States is not likely to be outvoted on this question in the near future. A sufficient number of UN members appears to be concerned about the future of Taiwan, and about Chinese use of force against India, to keep the Chinese representation issue stalemated for some time to come. It is interesting, however, that India continued to press for Chinese Communist representation in the UN while it was engaged in border fighting with the mainland Chinese.

A breakthrough on this question may have to await a basic shift in Communist Chinese attitude and policy or a significant shift in the attitudes toward China of a large number of UN member states. Major progress in disarmament negotiations could conceivably bring about such a change. For example, if a first-stage disarmament treaty appeared to be in the offing, the United States might feel compelled to urge Communist Chinese participation in the negotiations. Until such a time, any relaxation of U.S. official attitudes toward Communist China remains a highly controversial domestic political issue.

UNIVERSALITY OF MEMBERSHIP IN PRINCIPLE

The China question is obviously related in principle to such hypothetical questions as suspension of French and Russian voting privileges under Article 19 or a deliberate walkout from the UN of the Soviet Union, France or any other major power. The common principle is the willingness of these governments to accept what the majority of UN members may consider to be legal obligations under the Charter — in short, the competence of the full membership to define and enforce these obligations by vote. It also has a bearing on efforts to ostracize the Republic of South Africa from the UN.

Those who *defend* suspension of Assembly voting rights or expulsion do so on the grounds that only in these ways can the UN maintain both its integrity of purpose and (on the finance question) its administrative integrity. Unless violators of the rules are punished, the rules lose all meaning. Those who *oppose* such actions argue that purging the Organization of reluctant or recalcitrant nations (a) weakens the power base on which the effectiveness of the UN ultimately depends and (b) sanctions or even perpetuates a double-standard world — a law-abiding community (UN members who conform to majority rulings) and a lawless community (those who lose their vote or withdraw or are expelled and over whom the UN has abdicated its influence).

One further constitutional question — which has been raised but not widely debated — is whether a permanent member of the Security Council can withdraw or be expelled without rendering the Charter invalid. The five major powers are the only nations mentioned by name in the Charter (Article 23) and are assigned specific constitutional functions in the Security Council — permanent seat and veto — and in the Charter amendment process (Article 108). The question is whether these functions can legally be modified or withdrawn without Charter amendment.

CONTROVERSY OVER JURISDICTION

The problem of universality is also related to the jurisdictional issue — that is, the legal limits of the UN's competence to define or enforce binding obligations on member nations or to interfere in matters which members may consider to be their exclusive domestic concern.

Efforts to expel the Republic of South Africa from the UN, for example, are based on two propositions: (a) that South Africa's policy of *apartheid,* or separate development of white and nonwhite populations within its borders, constitutes both a violation of the principles of the Charter and a serious threat to the peace in Africa and (b) that South Africa's refusal to accept UN trusteeship responsibilities over the territory of Southwest Africa constitutes a persistent violation of the Charter within the meaning of Article 6. The South African government maintains, however, that both matters are "essentially within the domestic jurisdiction" of South Africa within the meaning of Article 2.

Similarly, Communist China insists that the status of Taiwan, and Peking's right to "liberate" the island, are matters of domestic jurisdiction and that any interference with this right, by the United States (which is allied to the Republic of China) or by the UN is illegal interference in China's internal affairs.

France opposes the General Assembly's past peace-keeping assessments on the grounds that they are illegal under the Charter and in violation of the sovereign rights of members: "by claiming the right to impose on the member states, including those opposed to it, financial obligations on the basis of a majority decision, the Assembly has given itself the attributions of a world government."

DOMESTIC JURISDICTION VERSUS WORLD AUTHORITY

Traditional concepts of national sovereignty reserve to each nation exclusive jurisdiction over domestic or internal affairs. Indeed, this exclusive domestic jurisdiction is a fundamental attribute of a sovereign nation and is so recognized in the UN Charter and the Statute of the International Court of Justice.

Yet, in a world without universal law — or impartial and objective interpretation of international law — each nation remains its own judge of what is or is not a "domestic" matter. And, in the contemporary international power system, the effectiveness of the UN — in a specific crisis and in basic principle — depends on clear definition of the distinction between *rights* of domestic jurisdiction and *duties and obligations* under the Charter.

The Statute of the International Court of Justice defines the jurisdiction of the Court to include "all cases which the parties [nations] refer to it and all matters especially provided for in the Charter of the United Nations or in treaties and conventions in force" (Article 36 of the Statute). The Charter specifically prohibits the UN (which includes the Court) from intervening "in matters which are essentially within the domestic jurisdiction of any state" except in peace-enforcement cases (Article 2, paragraph 7 of the Charter). Some nations, including the United States, have adopted legislation to reinforce their claim of exclusive right to distinguish between "domestic" and "international" affairs. However, the Statute of the Court (Article 36) invites all nations to "declare that they recognize as compulsory *ipso facto* and without special agreement" the Court's jurisdiction in certain broad areas. This is an invitation that has not been widely accepted.

Domestic jurisdiction is an old, not a new, problem. It remained undefined through 26 years of League of Nations practice and, after 18 years of UN operations, it is little closer to resolution. Yet it is a critical problem if the UN is to exert effective influence in the peaceful resolution of disputes.

DOMESTIC JURISDICTION AND POTENTIAL THREATS TO THE PEACE

Throughout most of the seven-year Algerian rebellion, France insisted that Algeria was an integral part of the French nation and that the rebellion was exclusively a domestic affair in which the UN had no right to intervene. Yet several Arab nations, the Soviet Union and even Communist China became directly involved in aid to the rebels. France found itself in diplomatic conflict and armed border incidents with Morocco and Tunisia and, at one stage, there was fear that the rebellion could erupt into a larger conflict, involving all of North Africa and perhaps even U.S. and Communist-bloc forces. The United States was inescapably involved in the problem, partly because France was using in Algeria U.S.-made military equipment and French troops that were nominally committed to NATO. The dilemma was not overcome until France explicitly recognized Algeria's right to self-determination. The truce then paved the way to Algerian independence in July 1962.

Portugal still insists on the domestic jurisdiction principle in connection with its African colony of Angola, where rebellious forces are receiving assistance from Algeria, the Congo and other African nations. Should this rebellion erupt into major violence, the UN membership would find itself divided on the issue of intervention in Angola. Prevailing sentiment in recent UN debates on Angola suggests that a substantial majority would favor UN intervention regardless of Portugal's claims of domestic jurisdiction. In the Security Council, however, there is still the possibility of a veto by any of Portugal's three NATO allies — the United States, Britain or France.

An equally dangerous problem may be fermenting in Southwest Africa, a former imperial German colony which after World War I was mandated (under Article 22 of the League of Nations Covenant) to what is now the Republic of South Africa. Southwest Africa was designated a "class C" mandate, one of those territories to be administered as "integral portions" of the territory of the mandate power. However, the League (and then its successor, the UN) retained certain supervisory responsibilities to insure the mandate was administered for the welfare of the indigenous population. Not only has the Republic of South Africa refused to recognize UN supervisory responsibilities for the former mandate (now trust territory) of Southwest Africa, it has also introduced its racial policies into the territory. Thus it has created an explosive situation of deep concern to the predominantly black nations of Africa as well as to other peoples of the world.

DOMESTIC JURISDICTION AND COLD WAR

The cold war has created wholly new and complex questions of what constitutes "intervention" — by the UN or by another nation — in the domestic affairs of a particular state.

The intervention of major powers in the internal affairs of lesser powers is no new phenomenon in history. Yet the cold war has elevated this practice to the level of fundamental strategic policy. Indeed, Communist ideology has given it the status of major doctrine. Peaceful coexistence, in Moscow's current terms, does not exclude "just wars" and "wars of national liberation," in which it is the responsibility of international communism to assist, and even to lead, the worker and peasant classes that are struggling for independence from either foreign or domestic tyranny. These missions are deemed necessary historical steps in the achievement of world communism.

On the other side in these same struggles, the United States and its allies are lending financial and military aid to what they consider to be democratic governments or factions, or to constitutional (if not democratic) regimes, or to regimes whose chief recommendation is that they are anti-Communist.

UN AND COLD WAR INTERVENTIONISM

Although the UN has so far had only marginal involvement in such battlegrounds for cold war intervention as Laos and South Vietnam, the international organization was caught in the middle of conflicting cold war strategies in the Congo. Various nations, at various times, condemned the UN for "intervention" in the domestic affairs of the Congo. The Soviet Union raised this complaint when the UN interfered with Soviet military aid to Lumumba's anti-Western, pro-Communist forces. Britain, Belgium and France raised the same complaint when the UN resorted to a show of force in order to influence secessionist Katanga province to accept the authority of the Congo central government. Concern was also expressed in Western Europe and the United States for self-determination of the people of Katanga—in other words, UN intervention in the "internal affairs" of Katanga.

It is important to recognize that UN Secretary General Thant ordered full-scale military action against hold-out Katanga troops only when he had open diplomatic support from the United States and at least tacit support from the Soviet Union. This suggests that how much "intervention" the UN has been able to undertake in a given situation has sometimes depended on political rather than strictly legal considerations.

There are innumerable other, less obvious areas in which the rights of domestic jurisdiction may run into serious conflict with the effective authority of the UN in preserving peace and order. One unresolved question, for example, is the limits of UN jurisdiction over individuals — local politicians, militia or civilians — who attempt to obstruct a peace-force operation. There is also some question whether civil rights, human rights and the rights of the individual person can be considered wholly "domestic" problems in this shrinking world. Certainly all these internal problems, in the United States as well as the Soviet Union and South Africa, have grave impact far beyond national borders.

As you noted earlier, the constitutional questions of universality of UN membership and scope of UN jurisdiction are being dealt with in the political arena. Whether these questions are resolved, or are temporarily swept under the rug, the process for doing so will be political. The dissenting nations will have to weigh the cost and consequences of continuing dissent; the UN majority will have to weigh the cost and consequence of demanding compliance. The future effectiveness of the UN, as it is now constituted, weighs in the balance of these political negotiations and contests of conviction.

ALTERNATIVES TO THE PRESENT SYSTEM

It is theoretically possible, of course, to retreat from the present UN system — that is, for a significant number of major powers to abandon the UN as a failure and, as a consequence, for the UN to follow the League into uselessness. In practical terms, however, it is difficult to imagine the total collapse of an international organization on which so many nations, especially new nations — and so many peoples — have pinned their hopes for a more stable world order.

It is also theoretically possible to surmount the present difficulties of the Organization and to emerge with a more effective world authority that is still tolerable to all concerned — either because of or in spite of its greater effectiveness.

One possibility is for a firm and consistent political stand on the part of those nations — possibly a substantial majority of the UN membership — that are committed to a "constitutional evolution" of the Organization in the direction of a more effective world authority. Conceivably, the demonstration effect of such a commitment could outweigh, and perhaps eventually overcome, the resistance of those nations that dissent from this commitment. The threat of indefinite isolation from the mainstream of international cooperation, in the UN, might weaken the resistance of dissenting major powers such as France and the Soviet Union over a period of time.

Another possibility is a giant step by all or nearly all of the world community of nations in the direction of a wholly reconstituted world authority — a vastly strengthened UN or a wholly new institution — which would offer the inducements, safeguards and checks and balances that would satisfy the most serious opposing concerns which make current controversies difficult to resolve. The time may come, in other words, when the risks to international stability that are inherent in the UN's present constitutional impasse prove less tolerable than an effective world authority which infringes somewhat on traditional national rights but which compensates for this infringement by guaranteeing national security within a framework of international stability.

This is the prospect that Clark and Sohn address themselves to in their proposals. Whether their plan can deliver on so complex an objective is less important than the fact that it opens up some useful lines of inquiry.

CLARK-SOHN PROPOSALS ON UNIVERSALITY AND JURISDICTION

The essence of the Clark-Sohn plan is the creation of a limited body of *world law* in an area where present *international law* is recognized as inadequate—that is, in the area of maintaining peace, preventing war and providing for the peaceful management of change in the world. The main purpose of the proposed new world law would be to make universal disarmament possible and enforceable.

These broad objectives, in the view of Clark and Sohn, require extensive machinery to legislate, apply and enforce the world law and to provide for peaceful change. They have framed their plan in terms of proposed revisions to the present UN Charter, although the total "model" would stand regardless of whether it was called "United Nations" or something else.

Essentially, the plan calls for extensive revision of present UN membership qualifications and admission procedures. It also calls for radical revision of the powers, composition and method of voting in the General Assembly to permit that body to legislate and implement the limited degree of world law which the authors believe disarmament demands. The peace-keeping authority of the new UN would be *universal.* The UN would also have clearly defined *jurisdiction* over the activities of all nations and peoples, whether members or not, on any matter related to the maintenance of peace. (The UN already has some authority over non-members in the peace-keeping field— Article 2, paragraph 6.)

UNIVERSALITY OF MEMBERSHIP

Under the proposed Charter revision, virtually the entire world would have to accept membership before the revision could go into effect. The intent is to obtain near unanimity for an admittedly radical restructuring of the world system. Thus ratification by five-sixths of the world's nations (including the twelve most populous nations) would be required. In addition, Clark and Sohn propose the following modifications regarding membership:

1. Legal status as an independent nation would be the only qualification for membership (rather than that the state be "peace-loving" and that it be "able and willing to carry out" its Charter obligations). Any dispute over an applying nation's legal status would be referred to the International Court of Justice for decision rather than to any political body. Barring a dispute, applications for membership would be honored automatically— without voting or veto.

2. There would be no possibility of withdrawal by or expulsion of any member nation, although as at present (Article 5) it would be possible to suspend temporarily the rights and privileges of a member against which the UN is engaged in a "preventive or enforcement action."

3. All nations and territories *not* members of the new UN would be required to comply with the "prohibitions and obligations of the disarmament plan" although they would not be compelled to support or participate in other UN programs.

Only on terms such as these, Clark and Sohn reason, would it be possible to obtain and maintain enforceable, universal disarmament: the enforcement authority (the UN) would have to command universal adherence to the disarmament provisions.

POWERS AND JURISDICTION OF GENERAL ASSEMBLY

The second radical revision which Clark and Sohn feel necessary is to lodge "final responsibility for the enforcement of the disarmament process and the maintenance of peace" with the General Assembly. They spell out what they believe to be adequate legislative and enforcement powers to insure the reliability of disarmament. And, in view of these vastly enlarged powers they would lodge with the General Assembly, Clark and Sohn propose a basic change in voting methods. In place of today's "one nation, one vote" pattern they propose weighted representation on a population basis, reminiscent of membership and voting in the U.S. House of Representatives.

The General Assembly's powers, however, would be strictly limited to areas related to the maintenance of peace. The General Assembly would have no power to regulate trade or immigration, for example, nor would it be permitted to intervene in the domestic affairs of any nation except to enforce disarmament or prevent international violence. In this area it would have power to regulate the conduct of individuals. The traditional rights of national sovereignty would disappear in all areas related to the use of force.

The plan calls for a clear distinction to be made between the General Assembly's powers of *recommendation* (which it now has, and which it would retain on a broadened basis), and its powers of *legislation* (which would be an innovation and would be carefully spelled out in the revised Charter and its various annexes). All powers not specifically delegated to the General Assembly would be reserved to the nations and their peoples.

Among the specific powers Clark and Sohn would give the strengthened General Assembly are the following:

1. Power to "enact laws and regulations . . . relating to universal, enforceable and complete national disarmament, including the control of nuclear energy and the use of outer space."

2. Power to establish laws and regulations related to enforcement of disarmament, including the establishment of a UN peace force (described in Session III).

3. Power to define crimes against the peace-keeping authority, to prescribe penalties for individual violators and sanctions for government violators, to apprehend and try violators—but only in the area of maintaining peace and preventing international violence.

4. Power to enact legislation to provide "sufficient and reliable revenues" to maintain the peace-enforcement authority, and to borrow money on the UN's credit for this purpose. (See Session IV.)

Thus, to the principle of universal authority Clark and Sohn would add the principle of clearly defined UN jurisdiction over all matters related to enforcing disarmament and maintaining peace. They would also add the power to raise "sufficient and reliable revenues" to insure the system against collapse.

(Seminar participants interested in the Clark-Sohn proposals for revising composition and voting procedures of the General Assembly will find these formulas detailed in *World Peace Through World Law,* pp. 25-34.)

LOOKING AHEAD

The range of political possibilities for constructing an effective world peace-keeping authority is, in other words, wide. Current UN controversies on constitutional questions such as the establishment of peace forces, binding financial obligations, universal membership and scope of jurisdiction all have an immediate as well as a long-term bearing on this problem. Perhaps the most important immediate question is, What can UN member nations do now to help move the Organization in the directions that will best serve the requirements of international peace and stability?

SUGGESTED READINGS:

MENDLOVITZ, pp. 184-234.
CLARK AND SOHN, pp. xvii-xxii and 1-65.

ADDITIONAL READINGS:

ABI-SAAB, GEORGE M. "The Newly Independent States and the Scope of Domestic Jurisdiction." *Proc. Am. Soc. Int. Law* 54: 84-90 (1960).

BRIGGS, HERBERT W. "The United States and the International Court of Justice: A Re-examination." *Am. J. Int. Law* 53: 301-318 (Apr. 1959).

BOWLES, CHESTER. "The China Problem Reconsidered." *Foreign Affairs* 38: 476-486 (Apr. 1960).

"Intervention Under the Charter of the UN and Under the Charter of the Organization of American States." *Proc. Am. Soc. Int. L.* 1957: 79-116.

WILCOX, FRANCIS O. U. S. Senate, Subcommittee on the UN Charter, Committee on Foreign Relations, 83rd Congress, 2nd Session, "Representation and Voting in the UN General Assembly. Washington: 1954.

WRIGHT, QUINCY. "The Goa Incident." *Am. J. Int. L.* 56: 617-632 (July, 1962).

REFERENCES:

ALWAN, MOHAMED. *Algeria Before the United Nations.* NY: Robert Speller, 1959.

FAWCETT, J. E. S. "Intervention in International Law." *Recueil des Cours* 103: 344-423 (1961, II).

GROSS, LEO. "Progress Towards Universality of Membership in the UN." *Am. J. Int. Law* 50: 791-827 (Oct. 1956).

HOWELL, JOHN M. and ROBERT R. WILSON. "The Commonwealth and Domestic Jurisdiction." *Am. J. Int. Law* 55: 29-44 (Jan. 1961).

KOROWICZ, MAREK. "Some Present Aspects of Sovereignty in International Law." *Recueil des Cours* 102: 1-119 (1961, I).

U. S. SENATE COMMITTEE ON FOREIGN RELATIONS. Subcommittee on the UN Charter. "Human Rights, Domestic Jurisdiction and the UN Charter." *Staff Study No. 11,* Washington; 1955.

WRIGHT, QUINCY. "Domestic Jurisdiction as a Limit on National and Supra-National Action." *Northwestern Law R.* 56: 11-40 (Mar.-Apr., 1961).

Session Five   QUESTIONS FOR REFLECTION OR
DISCUSSION

1. Is universality important to an effective UN?

To what extent and how would the effectiveness of the UN be impaired if the Soviet Union withdrew? if France withdrew? if the United States withdrew?

Is the effectiveness of the UN limited by the fact that Communist China is not represented in the Organization? Why or why not?

Should membership in the UN be considered a privilege, with obligations and responsibilities? If not, how can the UN set standards or influence international conduct? If so, and some nations are denied membership, how can the UN carry out universal responsibilities? Can this dilemma be resolved?

Would it impair the UN's effectiveness if South Africa were expelled on account of its *apartheid* policy and its policy toward Southwest Africa?

2. What jurisdictions does the UN need to be effective?

Should the UN assert the authority to intervene in the disputed trust territory of Southwest Africa in order to insure the rights of the indigenous population? Would this be interference in the internal affairs of the Republic of South Africa?

In the event of hostilities between South Africa and a group of tropical African nations, the UN would of course have the authority, under the Charter, to intervene in order to restore peace. In such an event, should the UN also assert the authority to remove a basic cause of the conflict—that is, to force South Africa to abandon its *apartheid* policy? Why or why not?

Under what circumstances, if any, should the UN interfere in domestic matters which constitute a threat to the peace? Should it have some power to regulate the conduct of individuals? Do you feel the UN exceeded its proper authority when it used force to influence the outcome of the problem of Katanga's secession? Why or why not?

Should the limits to the UN's jurisdiction in any specific breach of the peace be determined by legal principles or by political decision? Why?

SUMMARY QUESTION:

Do you believe it is possible for the UN to operate effectively in the maintenance of international peace as long as it lacks the authority to enact and the power to enforce laws dealing with war-prevention? If the UN were to acquire this authority and power, what limits should be placed on the UN's jurisdiction?

FRANCE, THE SOVIET UNION AND A FEW OTHER nations favor a narrow interpretation of the UN Charter — a "strict construction." They also favor political restraints on any evolution or enlargement of the Organization's powers under the Charter. Moreover, as you have seen in earlier sessions, they are willing to defy majority political decisions which they consider illegal. They view the UN (in Secretary General Hammarskjold's words) as little more than "static conference machinery," an intergovernmental institution with minimum power to bind the actions of its members and no power to bind or coerce any one of the five major nations.

The basis for this view is a narrow interpretation of those sections of the Charter specifying the powers of the principal organs, especially the General Assembly, Security Council and International Court of Justice. The UN, it is said, has no legislative, executive or judicial powers. The Organization's peace-keeping authority, under the narrowest interpretation of the Charter, rests with the Security Council and is therefore subject to great-power veto. According to this constitutional theory, the General Assembly has no authority to authorize the establishment or assess the costs of UN police actions; these are Security Council prerogatives. The Assembly's acceptance of the International Court's advisory opinion in December 1962 and its favorable vote on the seven financing resolutions in the resumed session in June 1963 have no legal force.

The key question is whether the Assembly majority, in voting on these matters, was actually "legislating" powers for itself in a manner not prescribed in the Charter.

A significant majority of the UN members, however, view the Organization and the Charter in a much broader light—(again in Hammarskjold's words) as a "dynamic instrument of Governments . . .

envisaging the possibility of continued growth toward increasingly effective forms of active international cooperation. . . ."

According to this interpretation, the Charter is not constrictive; it does allow for new powers to evolve constitutionally, with the consent of the membership, and in conformity with the intent and purposes of the Charter. Furthermore, most UN members accept the role that precedent performs in this constitutional evolution: when the membership *accepts* and *makes use of* enlarged powers of the General Assembly or Secretary-General, then these powers acquire a legal construction through the sanction of precedent.

In this session you will examine this constitutional evolution in the UN, various alternative proposals for restraining or strengthening the process, and some proposals for a radical restructuring of the UN and the creation of an effective world legislative and executive authority.

CHANGING ROLE OF THE SECRETARY-GENERAL

The emergence of the Secretary-General as the key figure in UN crisis diplomacy is one of the most interesting—and controversial—developments in the Organization's 18-year history. Successively under Secretaries General Trygve Lie, Dag Hammarskjold and U Thant, the influence of the UN's chief administrative officer has steadily enlarged. In the cases of Lie and Hammarskjold, the trend aroused the bitter personal animosity of the Soviet government. Hammarskjold and Thant were also severely criticized for their policies in the Congo crisis by Britain, France, Belgium and several African countries. The initiatives and growing influence of the Secretary-General are not universally condoned, in other words.

There are a number of explanations for this expanding role. One is the growth in UN membership and the multiplication of administrative, technical and diplomatic burdens thrust onto the Secretary-General by individual nations, groups of nations and several UN organs. Another is the failure of the Security Council to make Chapter VII of the Charter operative. In the absence of an effective Military Staff Committee and stand-by national military units on call to the Council, the Secretary-General has been charged with recruitment and direction of past UN peace forces. Perhaps most important, rivalries and deadlocks in both the Security Council and General Assembly—and the inability of either organ to formulate precise instructions on the political direction of peace forces—have left to the Secretary-General the day-to-day guidance of such complex and controversial UN operations as ONUC.

Furthermore, in dangerous situations such as the Cuban missile crisis, when traditional diplomatic channels and negotiations in the Security Council have threatened to break down, the Secretary-General has performed invaluable services as a neutral mediator representing the concerns of the rest of the world community. (It should also be noted that the growth in importance of the office is a reflection of the stature, competence and initiative of the three men who have occupied it.)

CONSTITUTIONAL POWERS OF SECRETARY-GENERAL

The Secretariat, of which the Secretary-General is chief executive officer, is one of the six principal organs of the UN. This status is significant, for the Secretary-General (like the General Assembly) is specifically authorized to "bring to the attention of the Security Council any matter which in his opinion may threaten the maintenance of international peace and security" (Article 99). The Congo crisis was the first matter brought before the Security Council by the Secretary-General under this article (July 1960). A derivative power, defined and exercised by Hammarskjold, allows the Secretary-General to make independent observations and investigations of crisis situations, either in person or through a personal representative or "presence." Secretary General Lie once pointed out that Article 99 "confers upon the Secretary-General . . . world political responsibilities which no individual, no representative of a single nation, ever had before."

Other powers and responsibilities specifically noted in the Charter include carrying out functions entrusted to him by the General Assembly and the Security, Economic and Social, and Trusteeship councils; making annual reports to the General Assembly, and administering the Secretariat.

INTERNATIONAL CIVIL SERVICE

Perhaps the most important doctrine in the Charter relating to the office of Secretary-General and the Secretariat is contained in Article 100:

1. "In the performance of their duties the Secretary-General and the staff shall not seek or receive instructions from any government or from any other authority external to the Organization. They shall refrain from any action which might reflect on their position as international officials responsible only to the Organization.

2. "Each Member [nation] of the United Nations undertakes to respect the exclusively international character of the responsibilities of the Secretary-General and the staff and not to seek to influence them in the discharge of their responsibilities."

This doctrine, which lays the foundations for an international civil service directed by an impartial executive officer, is supplemented by a further provision in the Charter: "The paramount consideration in the employment of [Secretariat] staff and in the determination of the conditions of service shall be the necessity of securing the highest standards of efficiency, competence and integrity. Due regard shall be paid to the importance of recruiting the staff on as wide a geographical basis as possible" (Article 101, paragraph 3).

The importance of these related Charter provisions is that they define an *international* responsibility above and beyond the interests of individual member nations. The Secretariat is conceived, in these two Articles, to be international rather than intergovernmental. In this sense the UN acquires what Hammarskjold called an "independent influence," subject only to the Charter and the consent of member nations.

IMPARTIALITY IN UN DIPLOMACY

Hammarskjold carried this doctrine into UN diplomacy. His function as an international civil servant, as he saw it, was to represent impartially the interests of the world community as these interests found expression in the UN. The initiatives authorized him under Article 99 and the responsibilities entrusted to him by the Security Council, General Assembly or other organs, were to be carried out in this spirit. He was to be guided, not by the simple facts of great-power—especially superpower—politics, but by the common interests and aspirations of all powers, great and small.

He recognized explicitly that this was a difficult role to perform when the major powers felt their vital interests were at stake, or when cold war issues were involved. It was impossible to ignore the realities of the existing power system. Yet, in crisis situations such as Suez and the Congo, Hammarskjold attempted to carry out policies reflecting the general will of the membership even when this required him to defy or ignore the will of major powers or important groups of nations— Britain, France, and Belgium; the Soviet Union and Casablanca powers (United Arab Republic, Morocco, Ghana, Guinea and Mali); and, on occasion, the United States.

In addition, Hammarskjold inaugurated a kind of quiet "preventive diplomacy"—behind-scenes discussions (rather than negotiations) intended to work out the basis for cooperation or negotiation of an incipient problem before the conflict erupted in open diplomacy and before the conflicting positions of governments hardened.

Hammarskjold considered it a duty for the Secretary-General "to use his office and, indeed, the machinery of the Organization to its utmost capacity and to the full extent permitted at each stage by practical circumstances. . . . The Secretary-General also should be expected to act without any guidance from the Assembly or the Security Council should this appear to him necessary towards helping to fill any vacuum that may appear in the systems which the Charter and traditional diplomacy provide for the safeguarding of peace and security."

The effect of these initiatives was to bring the Secretary-General under personal attack and the doctrine of impartiality into dispute.

IMPARTIALITY AND POWER POLITICS

The doctrine of impartiality has come under fire from the Soviet Union, which insists there can be no "neutral" individuals (even though Moscow was willing to accept neutral UN "verification" of the removal of Russian offensive weapons from Cuba in 1962). The doctrine has also been denigrated by other governments, including the French, as an excuse for illegal initiatives by the Secretariat. The controversy, in other words, reflects fundamental differences in attitude toward the Charter and the UN, whether the Organization is to perform as "static conference machinery" or as a "dynamic instrument of governments." Put in other terms, it is a dispute whether the UN should be a passive reflection of the existing international power system or whether it should provide creative opportunities for transcending the power system.

The conflict would exist even if a Secretary-General were to take no special initiatives. If he were to do no more than literally carry out the functions "entrusted to him" by other UN organs, experience demonstrates that he would still be unable to obtain clear and unambiguous instructions. The Congo operation was a classic case. To fail to act would be to fail in his entrusted responsibilities; to act at all is to act contrary to the will of one or more members of the Security Council or the General Assembly.

Those governments which favor a strict construction of the Charter apparently prefer "impartial inaction" to any UN action which threatens their own freedom of action.

EXECUTIVE ACTION IN THE SECURITY COUNCIL

A basic cause of the conflict over the Secretary-General's constitutional powers and responsibilities is the failure of the Security Council to perform the executive functions assigned to it in the Charter.

The original intent of the framers of the Charter—and certainly the vision shared at Yalta by Prime Minister Churchill, President Roosevelt and Generalissimo Stalin—was that the five great powers should serve as a continuing directorate for the international community as organized in the UN. Reflecting this concept, the Charter-framers assigned to the Security Council "primary responsibility for the maintenance of international peace and security" (Article 24, paragraph 1). This was the supreme task for which the UN had been established in the first place. In addition, the five great powers were assigned permanent seats, with veto, on the Council.

Originally the veto was conceived as a device to *promote negotiation,* rather than to *obstruct action.* It was generally assumed that collective peace-enforcement action against any one of the five major powers would be wholly unrealistic through UN channels. In part, therefore, the veto was designed to protect the interests of the five major powers, singly or together, against collective action favored by a large numerical majority, even if this majority had the support of one or more great powers.

Furthermore, in breaches of the peace where there was a split among the great powers on what course of action to follow, the veto was intended to encourage negotiation among them. Presumably, the common desire to take action, plus the requirement of unanimity, would lead to a plan of action acceptable to all five great powers plus at least two of the six lesser powers represented on the Security Council (for a majority of seven).

Several developments were apparently not anticipated by the Charter-framers. One was the relative decline in military-political importance of three of the permanent "great powers"—Britain, Republic of China and France. Another unanticipated development was the 1950 Uniting for Peace Resolution, which undermined the "primary responsibility" of the Security Council in the peace-enforcement area. Underlying this second development was the way in which the veto had actually been used: to prevent Security Council action, rather than to induce great-power unanimity on actions to be taken.

The veto has been used (and almost exclusively by the Soviet Union) to block Security Council action (a) on new admissions to the UN, although this impasse was resolved by negotiations in 1955, and (b) on resolutions supported by one group of powers (usually Western) and opposed by another (usually the Soviet Union). The non-Communist great powers have normally controlled a sufficient number of votes in the Security Council so they have only rarely had to resort to the veto. This parliamentary advantage has also made it possible for the West to press issues to a vote and thus demonstrate "for the record" that the Soviet Union uses its veto to obstruct action which the West and others may consider desirable.

In the process, the Security Council has been unable to carry out the executive functions originally assigned to it. By default, these functions have been shifted principally to the Secretary-General, but also to the General Assembly and ad hoc committees of the membership such as the Secretary-General's Advisory Committee on the Congo.

STRENGTHENING THE UN EXECUTIVE

There are various proposals for dealing with the problem. One is *troika,* which would introduce the unanimity or veto principle into the office of Secretary-General on a three-bloc rather than a five-power basis. Chairman Khrushchev made this proposal to the General Assembly in 1960. Arguing that there are no universal moral standards, and therefore no genuinely neutral individuals, he called for three coequal, secretaries-general, representing the distinct "moralities" of the Communist, capitalist and uncommitted worlds.

The General Assembly rejected the *troika* proposal overwhelmingly, although the issue may be raised again when Secretary General Thant's five-year term expires in 1966. The plan would no doubt insure a kind of impartial executive initiative by requiring unanimity among the three secretaries-general on any policy line or action. It would not resolve the problem which has so frequently paralyzed the Security Council—inability to act for lack of agreement on a specific line of action.

Another way of dealing with the problem is to return in practice in the Security Council to the original principle behind the veto. For the non-Communist great powers this would mean greater restraint in introducing and debating in the Council issues that are clearly unacceptable to the Soviet Union. For the Soviet Union it would mean greater restraint and responsibility in its exercise of the veto and in its manipulation of issues clearly unacceptable to the West. For all members of the Council, and particularly the five great powers, it would mean a complete change in style—avoidance of propaganda diplomacy and the initiation of earnest and serious negotiation of major conflicts with the aim of reaching great-power unanimity whenever and wherever possible.

A "reform" in Security Council diplomacy might be accompanied by an enlargement of the Council, a proposal noted briefly in the previous session. Additional seats might be created for those areas in the world now grossly underrepresented—especially Africa and Asia—and permanent seats, with veto, might be established for such important powers as Brazil, India, Japan and Nigeria. Various such proposals are currently under study in an Assembly subcommittee.

The Security Council is composed of eleven members, five of them permanent (Britain, China, France, the Soviet Union and the United States), and six of them elected to two-year terms by the General Assembly. The nonpermanent members are supposed to be selected with due attention to their contributions to international peace and security and to "equitable geographic distribution" (Article 23, paragraph 1). By an imperfectly kept gentleman's agreement, the six nonpermanent seats have generally been divided among Western Europe, Eastern Europe, British Commonwealth, Afro-Asia and two seats to Latin America.

Of the two criteria for the selection of the six nonpermanent members of the Security Council, the first (contributions "to the maintenance of international peace and security") is now virtually ignored and the second ("equitable geographical distribution") is impossible to fulfill unless the number of seats on the Security Council is increased.

At the time of the signing of the Charter in 1945, there were only two independent nations in all of tropical Africa (Liberia and Ethiopia). By the end of 1962, there were twenty-six. In addition, four nations of North Africa had gained independence, four Middle Eastern states had been admitted to the UN and eleven Asian nations had been admitted. Africa and South and Southeast Asia are very much underrepresented on the Security Council. (Similar inequities may be observed in the Economic and Social Council and the Trusteeship Council which, like the Security Council, have had no increase in membership since they were set up in 1945.)

Yet none of these steps would solve the problem of *inaction* in the Security Council when great-power agreement in a serious clash of interests proved impossible. Revival of the original unanimity principle would unquestionably help protect the freedom of action of the great powers—the United States and others, as well as France and the Soviet Union. It would not, however, serve the interests of those nations— including the United States and most of the smaller powers—which favor a Security Council able to take "prompt and effective action" in any crisis, as called for in Article 24.

Nor would it serve the further evolution of the UN in the direction of a more dynamic international instrument under impartial administration.

SECURITY COUNCIL VERSUS GENERAL ASSEMBLY

The question of the transfer of executive responsibilities from the Security Council to the Secretary-General is quite distinct from the question of transfer of peace-enforcement initiatives from the Council to the Assembly. The basic reason for this second development, as you noted earlier, was the pattern of Soviet use of the veto—a pattern which other nations considered abusive and which they feared might frustrate the UN in some future threat to the peace. The mechanism for transferring the initiative to the General Assembly, in case of Security Council deadlock, was the Uniting for Peace Resolution, which the Assembly passed in 1950.

Although the Soviet Union has labeled the procedure "illegal," Moscow was prepared to invoke it during the 1958 Lebanese crisis. Even earlier, in 1956, the Soviet Union acquiesced in the Uniting for Peace procedure, to invoke an emergency session of the Assembly in order to overcome British and French vetoes in the Council. There is some basis for the view, therefore, that the Soviet Union has helped establish the precedent, just as it, France and other nations have acquiesced in the precedent of delegating extraordinary executive responsibilities to the Secretary-General. Nonetheless, the constitutional question remains: Was the Assembly's action, in voting itself this peace-enforcement power, a form of legislation which was not provided for in the Charter?

The Soviet Union and France are not alone in their concern over the effects of the Uniting for Peace procedure. A number of observers deplore the trend. Some argue that the General Assembly (which had grown to 111 members by mid-1963) is too unwieldy a body and, furthermore, that the new nations occasionally demonstrate woeful irresponsibility in complex and delicate political issues such as the Congo. Others believe that by-passing the Security Council in this fashion has tended to aggravate great-power differences, especially on cold war issues.

Many other observers, however—and perhaps a majority of the governments now represented in the UN—welcome the growing power of the General Assembly in the peace-keeping area. The trend is viewed as insurance that the UN *can* act in times of crisis, regardless of the will of any of the great powers, including the Soviet Union and the United States.

Some view Soviet use of the veto as wholly irresponsible or feel that Western diplomacy in the Security Council has been wholly unconstructive, and for either or both reasons these observers consider the General Assembly (however unwieldy) a far more reliable organ than the Council for maintaining world peace and security. Some detect a maturing sense of responsibility in the membership of the Assembly—even greater, perhaps, than the great powers sometimes display—and would like to see the Assembly evolve in the direction of a genuine world legislative authority.

WHAT FUTURE DIRECTIONS FOR THE UN?

The choice among these various alternatives depends, once again, on what it is the world wants the UN to be or to become. This is another way of asking what may be politically feasible in the way of reform of UN practices or revision of UN structure.

A stricter construction of the UN Charter, and a retreat from the process of constitutional evolution, could conceivably take place simply by tacit agreement among the five permanent members of the Security Council. It would be politically difficult and financially impossible for the other 100-odd members to expand the initiatives of the Secretary-General or enlarge the powers of the General Assembly in defiance of the five great powers. The veto, plus the fact that the five now furnish two-thirds of the Organization's budget, would be formidable obstacles to overcome. Besides, political realities, especially the U.S. commitment to a strengthened UN, rule out for the forseeable future any such development. The United States, normally with the support of Britain and the Republic of China, seems more likely to press for greater, rather than less, initiative in the Secretariat and the General Assembly.

The evolutionary course faces some obstacles. The financing resolutions passed by the resumed session of the General Assembly in June 1963 left open (as you noted in Session IV) the question of legal principles. France, the Soviet Union and other nations in arrears on peace-force costs were not asked to abandon their constitutional views on the Charter; they were asked to pay up simply to resolve the UN's financial crisis. Should they continue adamant on the underlying legal questions, the constitutional deadlock could continue indefinitely.

In political terms, however, it may be possible for the UN to preserve its initiative and increase its influence as a "dynamic instrument" without any clear resolution of the constitutional question—as long, that is, as the dissenting nations choose to remain in the Organization, whatever its "faults," rather than abandon it to pursue their own independent courses.

Any revision of the UN structure, as opposed to a reform in practices, would present the most formidable obstacles. A change in the size of the Security Council (or the Economic and Social or Trusteeship Council) would require Charter revision. So would *troika* or any variation of it, according to most authorities. A ratification of certain, even limited, legislative powers for the General Assembly would also require Charter revision.

Revision of the UN Charter calls for a two-thirds vote in the Assembly and ratification by two-thirds of all member governments, by their own constitutional processes, including all five permanent members of the Security Council. In short, Charter revision is subject to great-power veto.

It would seem unlikely, for example, that the UN could open up the single, narrow question of enlarging or modifying the membership of the Security Council without, at the same time, opening up all the other inequities and controversies over UN structure, procedure and policy which also could only be handled by Charter revision. These controversies include the functions and powers of the Secretary-General, the role of the General Assembly in maintaining peace and assessing the costs of peace-keeping operations, and many other questions.

In view of the number and complexity of these constitutional questions, it may prove difficult or impossible to achieve any simple Charter revisions, no matter how clear the need. Indeed, it may prove just as easy to aim for complete Charter revision and a restructuring of the whole international system.

TAKING THE 'GIANT STEP'

A strengthened UN (or successor institution) with effective legislative, executive and judicial powers would require a full-member conference for Charter revision, a "constitutional convention" of the world's sovereign nations, or the imposition of a new world charter or constitution by force. The event might take place as a result of the progressive stalemating or disintegration of the UN, as an act of universal statesmanship in the face of mounting dangers and frustrations, or in the aftermath of a cataclysmic war.

Whichever of these prospects appear most likely, there is certainly some utility in considering how such a world might look.

World political federation or confederation is, of course, one theoretical possibility and it has many advocates and a variety of blueprints (from loose confederation to unitary world government) among Western thinkers. A world Communist society, achieved by evolution or revolution, is also theoretically possible. For present purposes, however, the most useful model to examine is the Clark-Sohn plan, which is based fundamentally on the contemporary UN experience. The plan could be achieved by drastic UN Charter revision, or by the adoption or imposition of a wholly new world charter. It represents a giant step away from the present world power system and UN structure and it assumes, as a primary condition, the acceptance of general and complete disarmament under enforceable world law. Yet its provisions are intended to answer the obvious dangers and weaknesses of the contemporary system.

Critical evaluation of the Clark-Sohn plan should help clarify what one would like the UN—and the world—to be or become and, perhaps, some sense of how to get there.

LEGISLATIVE-EXECUTIVE RESPONSIBILITIES

The most important constitutional change which Clark and Sohn propose in the present UN system is the creation of genuine legislative and executive functions, supported by effective judicial processes and an effective world peace-enforcement arm.

Legislative functions would be lodged with a restructured General Assembly which, as you noted in the previous session, would be empowered to enact world law only in areas related to the maintenance of world peace—supervision and enforcement of universal disarmament, prevention of international violence, and maintenance of a reliable revenue system to insure the perpetuation of the world peace-keeping authority. Furthermore, voting would be weighted according to population (rather than in terms of the sovereign equality of all nation-states) and members of the General Assembly would be encouraged to vote as individuals, rather than on the instructions of their governments. Ultimately representatives would be elected by popular vote in their respective countries rather than appointed by governments. The principle of an international civil service, already explicit in the UN Charter, would be supplemented by "internationalized" legislators who would be expected to balance national and international interests in somewhat the same way that members of national parliaments are now expected to balance local and national interests.

Executive functions would be lodged with a restructured Security Council, which Clark and Sohn would rename "Executive Council," and which would be elected by and responsible to the General Assembly. It would be, in effect, an agent of the General Assembly, responsible for supervision of the disarmament process and control of the new UN Peace Force—a permanent world monopoly on military force, the make-up of which you examined in Session III. The present UN Military Staff Committee (made up of the chiefs-of-staff of the five *major* powers) would be replaced by a committee made up of five professional military commanders recruited from the *smaller* powers and under civilian control of the Executive Council.

The most important transformations in the make-up of the Executive Council would be (a) elimination of the great-power veto, (b) expansion of the membership from 11 to 17, and (c) election of the Council by the General Assembly from its own membership (rather than appointment by member governments, as at present). The Executive Council would have permanent members, as at present (but without veto). These, however, would be the four nations with the largest population—China, India, the Soviet Union and the United States. (Britain and France would lose their permanent seats on the Council.) Other members of the Council would be elected for four-year terms through a formula insuring fair representation for various groupings of nations on a population and geographic basis. Ideological considerations would be ignored. Furthermore, members of the Executive Council (like members of the General Assembly) would be instructed to vote as individuals, thus extending to the executive arm of the strengthened UN the impartial civil servant principle already present in the UN Secretariat.

A form of veto would be retained in that, *on important matters,* the required majority of 12 on the Executive Council would have to include a majority of the representatives from the large-population group and a majority from the small-population group of nations, according to the Clark-Sohn classification system. Finally, the Executive Council would be subject to dismissal by vote of nonconfidence on the part of the General Assembly.

COLLECTIVE EXECUTIVE BODY

Thus the legislative-executive structure of the UN, under the Clark-Sohn proposals, would differ significantly from the present UN method of operation. Executive responsibility for peace-keeping would reside with a collective body, the Executive Council, as originally intended under the UN Charter, which gave the Security Council primary responsibility in this field. The Secretary-General, under the Clark-Sohn plan, would not be the scapegoat for the Council's inability to provide clear and unambiguous instructions for day-to-day control of a police action. The proposed Executive Council, however, would no longer be a reflection of the great-power realities of 1945; it would be instead a body of individuals elected by, responsible to and dismissable by a General Assembly which, in turn, reflected the views of the world's peoples rather than the policies of sovereign, competitive and armed nation-states.

The Secretary-General would retain the same specific powers he now possesses under the UN Charter. Indeed, his powers under Article 99, to bring to the attention of the Security Council "any matter which in his opinion may threaten the maintenance of international peace and security," would be strengthened by being made mandatory rather than discretionary. But the vacuum-filling powers of the Secretary-General, which have evolved in practice, would presumably become far less significant. An internationalized cabinet or Executive Council—rather than the Secretary-General and his *ad hoc* committees—would be charged constitutionally with carrying out peace-enforcement decisions reached in the General Assembly.

The effect of these proposals would be, in Clark and Sohn's words, to transform the UN into "something very different from and more than a league of sovereign states represented by delegates selected by governments." The plan envisages, not only an international civil service such as now mans the Secretariat, but also the gradual creation of an international citizenship in which the enactment and enforcement of world law would be carried out by individuals responsive to the Charter, to the world community of peoples and to their own consciences rather than to distinct national interests. The plan envisages the emergence of a new breed of international statesmen to whom the world would entrust the enforcement of disarmament and the maintenance of world peace.

Basically this concept represents a substantial evolution beyond the concept of an impartial Secretary-General and the Secretariat made up of international civil servants—a new breed that is already in existence and is already exerting an independent influence in world diplomacy. The fundamental question, in other words, is one the world already faces: In what ways, and to what extent, should the independent influence of the UN be enlarged and expanded?

LOOKING AHEAD

This is not a mechanical question; rather, it lies at the crux of contemporary world politics. The UN acquires somewhat expanded influence each time it is entrusted with a new function—a peace-keeping operation, as in the Congo, an expanded technical assistance effort or a mission of quiet diplomacy in a great-power crisis. An inspected test ban or an agreement on peaceful uses of outer space might give some increased power to one or more UN organs—the Security Council, the General Assembly, the Secretary-General, or a new test-ban or disarmament agency linked to the UN system. A major arms control or disarmament plan would very possibly transfer to the UN some new prerogatives—inspection, enforcement and perhaps sanctions or punishment for violations.

In short, the UN is already a growing independent force. The question is whether, in what ways, or how far this trend should be encouraged and strengthened.

SUGGESTED READINGS:

MENDLOVITZ, pp. 237-302.

CLARK AND SOHN, pp. xxii-xxiv, 66-88, 183-186.

ADDITIONAL READINGS:

GOODRICH, LELAND M. "The Political Role of the Secretary-General." *Int. Org.* 16 (Autumn, 1962).

JACKSON, ELMORE. "Constitutional Developments of the UN: The Growth of Its Executive Capacity." *Proc. Am. Soc. Int. Law* 55: 78-88 (1961).

MUNRO, SIR LESLIE. "Recent Developments in the Role of the General Assembly in the Maintenance of Peace." *Proc. Am. Soc. Int. Law* 52: 34-47 (1958).

PADELFORD, NORMAN J. "Politics and Change in the Security Council." *Int. Org.* 14: 381-401 (Summer, 1960).

PETERSEN, KEITH S. "The Uses of the Uniting for Peace Resolution Since 1950." *Int. Org.* 13: 219-323 (Spring, 1959).

SCHACTER, OSCAR. "Dag Hammarskjold and the Relation of Law to Politics." *Am. J. Int. Law* 56: 1-8 (Jan. 1962).

SHARP, WALTER R. "Trends in UN Administration." *Int. Org.* 15: 393-407 (Summer, 1961).

WASHINGTON, GEORGE THOMAS. "Improvement of Organization for Collective Security—Alternatives to the Veto Power." *Proc. Am. Soc. Int. Law* 51: 127-134 (1957).

REFERENCES:

ALEXANDROWICZ, C. H. "The Secretary General of the United Nations." *Internatl. Comp. L. Q.* 11: 1109-30 (Oct. 1962).

GROSS, ERNEST A. *The United Nations: Structure for Peace.* NY: Harper, for the Council on Foreign Relations, 1962.

LASH, JOSEPH. *Dag Hammarskjold: Custodian of the Brush-Fire Peace.* NY: Doubleday, 1961.

LOVEDAY, ALEXANDER. *Reflections on International Administration.* Oxford: Clarendon Press, 1956.

U. S. Senate Committee on Foreign Relations. Subcommittee on the UN Charter. "The Status and Role of the Secretariat of the UN." *Staff Study No. 12*. Washington, 1955.

WILCOX, FRANCIS O. U. S. Senate, Subcommittee on the UN Charter, Committee on Foreign Relations. "The Problem of the Veto in the UN Security Council." 83rd Congress, 2nd Session, Washington, 1954.

YOUNG, TIEN CHENG. *International Civil Service: Principles and Problems*. Brussels: International Institute of Administrative Sciences, 1958.

Session Six   QUESTIONS FOR REFLECTION OR DISCUSSION

1. What is the proper role of the UN Secretary-General?

Do you consider that the vacuum-filling functions the Secretary-General has been performing are a demonstration of strengths—or weaknesses—in the UN? Why?

Is it possible, in your opinion, for an international civil servant to be impartial in carrying out his duties? If not, why not? If so, must there be certain conditions before he can successfully do so? Is there a difference between "impartiality" and "neutrality" — between objective application of legal or moral principles and indifference to these principles?

In the present power system, as it is reflected in the UN, can the Secretary-General be realistically expected to carry out executive responsibilities on behalf of the full membership? If so, in what sense? If not, why not? Should such responsibilities be thrust on the Secretary-General?

2. Where should executive responsibility lie among various UN organs?

Do you believe the Security Council, with its present membership, including the five permanent members, could carry out the executive functions assigned to it under the Charter? Why do you think it has failed to do so in the past? What reforms in Security Council member-ship, or in the practices of the present membership, would be necessary to insure that the Council could effectively fulfill its "primary responsi-bility for the maintenance of international peace and security"?

Do you believe the General Assembly can carry out this responsi-bility more effectively? How? In past peace-force operations, do you feel the General Assembly has demonstrated some weakness or irrespon-sibility in this field? Do you think it is constitutionally proper for the General Assembly to take the initiative in peace-keeping when the Secur-ity Council shows it is unable to act? Why or why not?

3.   *What are the alternatives to the present system?*

What would be the advantages and disadvantages of carrying out the inoperative Articles of Chapter VII — restoring primary responsi-bility for peace-enforcement to the Security Council?

Would there be any important advantages in expanding the mem-bership of the Security Council? If so, along what lines?

What are the advantages of continuing past trends — increased initiative on the part of the General Assembly and growing influence of the Secretary-General?

In your opinion, what are the merits or drawbacks of the Clark-Sohn proposal — lodging primary responsibility for peace-enforcement with the General Assembly and reconstituting the Security Council as an executive cabinet for the Assembly?

SUMMARY QUESTION:

What steps are desirable or necessary if the UN is to become an effective peace-enforcement authority — further evolution of the present system, a return to the original concept of the Charter-framers, substan-tial changes in the present membership and/or functions of the major UN organs, or a radical reconstruction of the whole UN system?

ONE OF THE GRAVEST DANGERS OF THE CONTEMPORARY international system is that deep conflicts in national aims and interests, and ideological competition, can erupt into war — and that war at the level modern weapons permit could be unprecedentedly devastating.

It is among the purposes of the UN to place legal restraints on the use of force, to provide and encourage the use of peaceful channels for the resolution of international disputes, and in the last resort to mobilize the collective power of nations in order to maintain or restore peace.

Yet, no matter how much independent influence the UN may exert in world politics, it lacks decisive military power in its own right. It can *mobilize legal force* for the purpose of *countering illegal force* only when it has the consent and military cooperation of its members.

Indeed, with the exception of Korea and, in the most limited sense, the Congo, no past UN show of force has been much more than symbolic. In short, the UN's powers, as an institution, are more moral and persuasive than coercive. As a collective security agency, its military powers are those delegated to it by an effective coalition within its membership. Its capacity to use force to maintain international peace and security rests on (a) its ability to borrow national power from its members and (b) assurance that its efforts will not be obstructed by the major powers, especially the two superpowers.

Thus, paradoxically, the UN's military power-base — its only resource for physically enforcing the peace — is the same competitive national military power which periodically threatens the peace.

It is important, therefore, to explore two further approaches to the control of violence and the maintenance of peace in international relations. One is to control or regulate national power within the existing international system — *arms control*. The other is to transform the existing system by eliminating national military power as the ultimate governing factor in international relations — *general and complete disarmament.*

In this session you will be concerned with the first of these two approaches: measures designed to stabilize or decelerate the arms race, to reduce the tensions and dangers arising from the arms race, or to regulate or even reduce arms levels without actually eliminating national armaments.

VARIETY OF ARMS CONTROL MEASURES

From a *procedural* point of view an arms control arrangement may come about from a formally negotiated agreement such as the recent limited nuclear test-ban treaty or an agreement on peaceful uses of outer space. Or it may arise from tacit agreement on both sides to observe certain restraints or to follow certain unwritten rules. An example of the latter is the tacit agreement among today's nuclear powers to discourage the spread of nuclear weapons technology to other powers.

From a *functional* point of view, arms control may consist of a first "confidence-building" step designed to relax arms-race tensions and pave the way toward a more comprehensive military (or even political) arrangement that helps secure the peace. Or it may be a measure to deal with an obvious technical or strategic problem such as accidental war or surprise attack. Or it may be a measure which actually introduces some degree of arms limitation and/or regulation.

Either procedure — tacit or formal — may involve various functional measures — confidence-building steps, technical measures, safeguards against surprise attack or reciprocal reductions in forces and weapons. A formal agreement would of course be required for arms regulation with verification and inspection. Finally, some arms control proposals are suggested as ends in themselves — as measures which will introduce an indefinite period of military stability — while other proposals are offered as purely transitional measures.

A useful place to begin is with tacit approaches to arms control since this category includes a variety of measures already in effect.

TACIT RESTRAINTS ALREADY IN EFFECT

The two superpowers have consistently observed a variety of unwritten rules and regulations which help make the arms race — and the hostile confrontation — somewhat less dangerous than it might otherwise be.

Nondispersal of nuclear weapons technology to other powers is one such unwritten rule. Neither the United States nor the Soviet Union, so far as is publicly known, has assisted any of its allies to acquire nuclear armaments. Wartime collaboration among the United States, Britain and Canada in the development of the first atomic bombs did lead to continuing U.S.-British arrangements for the exchange of information on nuclear technology, but Britain was already a charter member of the nuclear club. Neither the United States nor Britain assisted France to acquire nuclear capabilities and, on the diplomatic front, Washington has attempted to discourage the French initiative. Nuclear weapons belonging to both superpowers have been stationed on the territories of other nations — East and West Germany, Cuba, Turkey, Italy, etc. — but have presumably remained under superpower control.

The three major nuclear powers — the United States, Soviet Union and Britain — in short, have all tacitly acknowledged, at least to date, that it is in their common interest to prevent the spread of nuclear weapons insofar as this is possible. In mid-1963 this principle was expressed formally in the three-power limited test-ban treaty.

Another cautionary principle proclaimed on both sides is the need to perfect systems of command and control over their respective nuclear striking forces. The speed of highly destructive modern weapons underscores the importance of safeguards against human or mechanical error, or accidental or unauthorized firings. Both Moscow and Washington are officially committed to programs of this type and Washington has revealed in public some details of command and control safeguards already adopted. An important purpose of this publicity is to reassure the other side that the probabilities of accidental war are deliberately being reduced.

MUTUAL RESTRAINT IN CIVIL DEFENSE

There is another tacit restraint in effect in that both superpowers have so far avoided all-out civil defense programs. There is, of course a difference between a "survival-and-reconstruction" civil defense program and a "crash" program — between self-protective measures and measures that are so elaborate they are provocative. So far neither the United States nor, presumably, the Soviet Union has undertaken civil defense at more than a minimum level.

Some observers feel that a crash civil defense program on either side might be interpreted by the other side as a commitment to an aggressive military policy — perhaps even as preparation for a thermonuclear attack. Part of the reasoning is that neither superpower would divert enormous resources to civil defense unless it believed there was a high probability of being struck and that the one course of action that would insure being struck would be to strike first.

(There are, however, strong arguments for national civil defense programs that would help keep the loss of life and property to a minimum, and would protect essential resources for rebuilding the postwar society, in case major war should occur. Even admitting there is no effective way of protecting a civilian population that is the main target of a surprise thermonuclear attack, it is still important to realize that other targets — especially military bases — would be of far greater strategic importance than cities, either to an aggressor or to a retaliating victim. Therefore a civilian shelter program, combined with stockpiling of food, medicine and essential raw materials and machinery, could greatly reduce deaths from indirect causes such as radioactive fallout and could shorten enormously the time required to restore the society to prewar levels.)

TACIT RESTRAINT IN BUDGET AND FORCE LEVELS

Various proposals have been advanced for extending the area of tacit restraints observed by both sides. The unilateral reduction of military budgets, for example, in a period of relatively peaceful coexistence, has been suggested as a way of reducing tensions and — if the move is reciprocated — of paving the way toward further stabilization or deceleration of the arms race.

As a matter of historical record, budgetary cuts were made on both sides, together with reductions in forces, during the brief "spirit of Geneva" (1955-56) and "spirit of Camp David" (1959-60) periods —

following the Korean war and death of Stalin and preceding the aborted summit conference of May 1960.

While economy may have been the principal motive for the cuts, and while neither side admitted any weakening of its over-all military strength as a result of the cuts, there was the implication that the reductions might also help ease tensions. Historians differ in their judgments of the usefulness of such exercises. It may be argued, for example, that the resumed arms competition may be more intense, and more dangerous in its effects on diplomacy, if it follows a false lull in cold war competition.

Nonetheless, military budgets and force levels have a psychological impact — as well as strategic implications — and no doubt have an important place in any period of mutual probing. If the current series of East-West negotiations shows some promise of being constructive, the negotiating climate might be improved by a symbolic cut in defense spending. Conversely, an increase in defense spending, or a step-up in force levels, has been used on both sides in the past to signal dissatisfaction with the course of diplomatic negotiations or political developments.

MORATORIUMS AND PROHIBITIONS

The three-year Soviet-U.S.-British tacit moratorium on nuclear testing, which the Soviet Union breached in 1961, had both practical and symbolic effects. In practical terms it briefly slowed down the race in nuclear technology and arrested the hazards of radioactive fall-out from the tests. Symbolically, it temporarily raised hopes for success in the arms talks then under way (hopes that were later dashed). The unilateral U.S. ban on above-ground testing, announced in the spring of 1963, was made conditional on similar restraints by other nuclear powers. A few observers believe this U.S. moratorium may have improved the climate for the formal test-ban negotiations in Moscow, which followed during the summer. Others believe that the Soviet Union was already determined—for economic and political reasons—to obtain a treaty ban on all but underground tests and that the U.S. action was an acknowledgment of this rather than an effort to influence Soviet policy. In any event, the treaty was negotiated and signed and it opened the way for further East-West talks on outstanding military and political questions.

Generally speaking, the United States has shied away from informal moratoriums and prohibitions — including the Soviet proposal that nuclear weapons be declared "illegal." The Soviet Union, on the other hand, has often advocated the declaratory technique. Declarations such as these are useful, obviously, only to the extent that they are reciprocally observed. They are a form of self-enforcing arms control based on unilateral measures that are fully reciprocated or on bilateral announcements of a common policy. In fact, the 1963 Moscow treaty is also self-enforcing: it prohibits only those tests which can be detected by national intelligence techniques and it allows any government to withdraw unilaterally, after due notice, "if it decides that extraordinary events . . . have jeopardized [its] supreme interests."

'HOT-LINE' TELECOMMUNICATIONS AGREEMENT

Formal arrangements in the arms control field may range in complexity from the technical agreement setting up a "hot-line" telecommunications link between the White House and the Kremlin, through a verified and inspected nuclear test ban, to a treaty which limits and regulates arms levels.

The hot-line agreement, negotiated in June 1963, is designed primarily to insure reliable and rapid communications between the heads-of-government of the two superpowers in any future crisis situation. The Cuban missile crisis had demonstrated the difficulties, delays and dangers of relying on normal diplomatic channels (through respective embassies) and coded commercial cables in periods of deep tension. With the new direct-line equipment (and a standby microwave relay) two-way communication, including Russian-English translations, will be almost instantaneous.

The communications system is a form of arms control, not because it affects arms levels (which it does not), but because it can play a role in controlling the use — or nonuse — of force. In an age of quick-response weapons, it buys time for more cautious and more deliberate decision-making on both sides, thus reducing the danger of miscalculation, spasm response or accidental war. It may also be considered a confidence-building step in the sense that it is an electronic demonstration of the peaceful intentions of both sides.

STABILIZED DETERRENCE AS A FORM OF ARMS CONTROL

As you noted in Session I, there is widespread interest in the possibility that the superpower arms race may be entering a period of relatively stable deterrence. Viewed as an exercise in tacit arms control — informal mutual restraint — stabilized deterrence would have most of the following characteristics (especially the first three):

HIGHLY INVULNERABLE RETALIATORY FORCES.

Both sides should have an adequate number of second-strike weapons such as missiles buried and protected in hardened bases, or dispersed in submarines, surface ships or airborne bombers. These weapons must have the capacity to survive a first strike and to retaliate with unacceptable destructiveness on the initiator of a war.

LIMITED STRATEGIC FORCES.

The size of the retaliatory arsenal on each side should correspond realistically to its mission. If it is too small, it is not a credible deterrent — it would be vulnerable to a small number of direct hits in a first strike. But if it is too large, then it crosses a certain psychological threshold and appears provocative to the other side — it may even look like a first-strike threat.

FLEXIBLE CONVENTIONAL FORCES.

Both sides should have a military alternative to thermonuclear war. Adequate conventional military forces serve to demonstrate that a nation is willing to fight a small war and is able to keep it from becoming a major war.

RELATIVELY VULNERABLE POPULATION AND INDUSTRY.

Both sides should avoid the kind of crash civil defense effort which suggests it might be willing to risk major war as an instrument of policy. A vulnerable population serves as a demonstration of peaceful intentions.

LIMITED TECHNOLOGICAL EFFORT.

Defense spending, especially that part of it devoted to weapons research and development, should be small enough on both sides to demonstrate that neither side is trying to break the stalemate.

ADEQUATE MUTUAL INTELLIGENCE.

Although stable mutual deterrence is based on informal reciproca-
tion, rather than on a formal treaty with built-in inspection and verification devices, it does presume a high degree of mutual awareness, whether
through normal channels or espionage. Great secretiveness would be as
incompatible with stabilized deterrence as it would be with general and
complete disarmament. In fact, the foundation of stabilized deterrence
is continuing open demonstration by each side that it prefers stability to
resumption of an uncontrolled arms race.

ACCEPTABLE LEVELS OF DISCONTENT.

The political climate must also be favorable to continuing arms
stability. If either side feels sufficiently aggrieved, and is unable to gain
relief through diplomatic channels, it may decide that the risks of a resumed arms race are preferable to continued stalemate.

DIFFICULTIES OF ACHIEVING STABILITY

This is obviously a complex set of factors to achieve. For example,
how many invulnerable weapons does each side need in order to insure,
after a sneak attack, that it will be able to retaliate with sufficient destructiveness and, therefore, can deter the sneak attack in the first place?
At what point — 200, 500 or 1,000 retaliatory weapons — would one
side's "deterrent" become so huge that the other side considered it a first-
strike threat? At what force level — half a million, 1 million or 2 million
men — would one side's conventional military establishment be interpreted by the other side as a threat of non-nuclear aggression? Granted
that in a "honeymoon" period there might be strong motivations on both
sides to maintain arms stability, would such restraints survive a serious
political crisis or brush-fire war in, say, Africa or the Middle East, where
the interests of the superpowers were in direct conflict?

The numbers problem in missiles is particularly vexatious. From a
political point of view, the fewer missiles on each side, the smaller the
threat of aggression or sneak attack with weapons on hand. Yet, in
military terms a small number of missiles on each side makes the situation
potentially more dangerous. A small retaliatory arsenal could more easily
be canceled out by a technological breakthrough on the other side —

for example, vastly superior aiming accuracy or a highly efficient anti-missile missile. A large number of missiles on each side would also be preferable if present levels of secrecy were maintained. In that event, a few hidden missiles — or inaccurate intelligence estimates about the number of missiles on the other side — would not greatly alter the balance. The problem is not merely to reconcile political and military considerations on both sides, but also to determine *what risks* are tolerable to each side in order to make mutual stability *less risky* than an unlimited arms race.

In summary, mutual nuclear deterrence can be only as stable as the competitive pursuits of the two superpowers permit. It would require both sides to exercise much the same restraints that have so far helped keep the world from thermonuclear war — the restraints of mutual self-interest in avoiding dangerous provocations.

Mutually invulnerable retaliatory weapons may make it easier to slow down the arms race — but only as long as both sides consider it to be in their common interest to do so.

In the absence of arms parity, and in face of the apparent determination of the United States to preserve its superiority and of the Soviet Union to challenge this superiority, the arms race has tended to accelerate. It still remains to be seen whether the new generation of invulnerable weapons now coming into operation will influence this trend. It is also a matter of speculation whether the United States may, sometime in the future, accept a military balance that is closer to real parity — a highly controversial issue in U.S. policy circles. It may be that only on such terms will it be possible to think of stabilized deterrence as a workable form of arms control — with or without formal agreements.

STABILITY AT MINIMUM ARMS LEVELS: FINITE DETERRENCE

Conceivably, mutual nuclear deterrence could operate on the basis of substantial reductions in nuclear weapons levels on both sides — either by elaborate treaty or by simple mutual agreement on the levels of forces and armaments to be maintained. These levels would be set at the minimum military balance necessary for both sides to feel secure. If agreement were reached it could produce a controlled nuclear stalemate, or what is commonly called "finite deterrence" or "minimum deterrence."

The principal characteristic of finite deterrence is that it calls for a very small striking force on each side. In this sense it would differ from types of stabilized deterrence discussed earlier. Arms and force levels would be reduced below the threshold of an all-out war or massive-retaliation capacity. The number of missiles retained by each side would be as symmetrical as possible and would be intended, not for reciprocal devastation, but for punitive purposes — to punish the other side for an unacceptable provocation. Furthermore, the punishment would be limited and might even be understood or announced in advance — "if you make military move A, we will strike your city X with so many megatons; unless you withdraw your ultimatum B, we will destroy your industrial complex Y."

Another distinctive characteristic of finite deterrence is that it would emphasize civilian and industrial targets over military targets. This is an inevitable by-product of reducing striking forces to minimum levels. In an era of hardened, relatively invulnerable missiles, and less than precise target intelligence or aiming accuracy, a successful strike against a hardened missile base may require five or ten missiles per target. Thus a reliable "counterforce strategy" — a strategy based on a reasonable ability to knock out or cripple the enemy's striking power — requires a substantial missile *lead* over the enemy. Obviously this is an advantage which both sides cannot enjoy simultaneously.

A finite deterrent strategy is based on more or less the *same* number of highly invulnerable missiles on each side. Since neither side has a numerical advantage, it cannot be sure of knocking out the other side's missile bases. The only reasonable targets, therefore, are vulnerable civilian and industrial targets. Hence finite deterrence is a punitive counter-city strategy rather than a counterforce strategy.

Negotiating a finite deterrence arrangement might in some respects be more difficult than achieving a tacit stabilized deterrence. In the first place, finite deterrence requires negotiation and agreement on delicate and complex strategic points such as what constitutes a "minimum balance" in numbers of retaliatory missiles. Second, it involves a shift in targets — from military to civilian and industrial — which may appear to be cynical and inhumane, even though the purpose is to make any strike less likely. Also, it tends to limit national freedom of action at the non-nuclear level — it makes it possible to put a price tag of nuclear punishment on a conventional military provocation or even, conceivably, on an unacceptable political action.

Yet an analysis of the concept is useful because it points up the desirability of some sharper definition of the "rules of the game" in a competitive power system. It also points up the difficulties of an arms control plan based on the reduction of armaments and forces to minimum but still lethal levels.

ARMS CONTROL AS A TRANSITIONAL PROBLEM

Many experts have difficulty in thinking of any arms control measure as an end in itself. A limited first step, such as tacit reductions in arms budgets on both sides, or the formally negotiated hot-line arrangement, or even the 1963 self-enforcing treaty to ban all but underground nuclear tests, makes no real difference in the arms competition. It does not change the ground rules. It simply slows the arms race a bit or installs a new safety device to help prevent certain types of accidents.

Even stabilized deterrence — whether it evolves through technology and a tacit balancing of forces or whether it is formally negotiated at some finite or minimum level — may offer nothing more than a respite. A stable nuclear standoff would introduce some new self-enforcing ground rules but it would not amend the fundamental rules of the power competition. The arms confrontation would be modified, or brought into less nervous balance, but it would remain the ultimate governing factor in international relations.

Moreover, there is always the possibility that a particular arms control measure, once adopted, may expose or create an unforseen danger that cancels out the hoped-for benefits of the arrangement. Balanced cutbacks in one type of weapon may coincide with a technological breakthrough which makes another type of weapon suddenly more important. The arms race may simply shift fields and speed up instead of being slowed down. Any tampering with the existing military balance between the two superpowers (even if in the name of arms control) carries some risks. Finally, an arms control arrangement between the two superpowers may leave untouched — or only indirectly affect — the military competition among all the lesser powers.

For all these reasons, many experts insist on dealing with any arms control proposal as part of a process—a step in a long-term strategy of progressive stabilization or elimination of global arms competition. Thus a confidence-building step would be useful only if it were followed up by some further step which took advantage of whatever level of mutual confidence might have been achieved. The further step, in turn, should lead to broader negotiations and new stabilization measures based on the previous experiences. The three-power Moscow test-ban treaty, for example, tends to freeze certain types of large-scale nuclear weapons developments, including the development of an effective antimissile missile, although it does not preclude the underground testing of small, sophisticated nuclear weapons devices. (It also tends to limit the dispersal of nuclear technology to the extent that potential nuclear powers accede to the treaty.) Possible next steps might include political settlements (on the status of Berlin, for example) or further progress in banning nuclear tests, such as a verified and inspected ban on all tests, including underground tests. An inspected test-ban treaty, in turn, would provide opportunities for experimenting with certain inspection techniques which might be applicable to still more elaborate arms control measures or to general and complete disarmament.

There are, in fact, a number of arms control proposals which are largely transitional in purpose and function. These include an inspected test ban, demilitarization and disengagement.

INSPECTED NUCLEAR TEST-BAN TREATY

A treaty ban on *all* nuclear tests would perform several arms control functions. Most important, if effectively enforced it would arrest nuclear technology and hinder the dispersal of nuclear capabilities to other nations. It would not prevent laboratory and theoretical work on advanced weapons, but it would prevent all testing—and therefore the perfecting — of new weapons. Thus if the agreement were to collapse after it had been in force for some time, nuclear weapons technology would be picked up at more or less the cut-off point rather than at some highly advanced, and therefore more dangerous, level.

One of the greatest hazards of an uncontrolled arms race is that weapons technology seems to progress much faster than reliable methods for controlling armaments. The proliferation of nuclear warheads in the late 1950's and early 1960's, for example, rules out the kind of reliable arms-control inventory of weapons-in-being that might have been possible in the 1940's. In fact, some observers fear that unless a universal nuclear test-ban treaty is negotiated in the next few years, the military art may progress to the point where enforceable disarmament — let alone an enforceable test ban — will become impossible without police-state surveillance on a global scale. Therefore even a temporary "freezing" of technology is considered by most experts to be highly desirable.

In addition, an inspected nuclear test ban would provide an opportunity to experiment with various types of verification and inspection machinery — seismic devices, neutral verification and inspection teams, data analysis and other procedures that might be applicable to more elaborate arms control arrangements or to a plan for general and complete disarmament.

This suggests that a workable test-ban treaty would also be a confidence-building measure. In addition to the important benefit of limiting the development and spread of nuclear technology, it could help pave the way toward more extensive efforts to regulate armaments. For this reason U.S. and British experts have been willing to accept some risks — such as fewer on-site inspections than they consider desirable or ideal — simply to get a workable agreement. They consider the dangers of no agreement to be far greater than the risks of a few undetected Soviet underground tests. Some of the same arguments are used to justify the uninspected ban on above-ground tests.

It is important to point out that a completely foolproof inspection system for an underground test ban is considered technically as well as politically infeasible by many experts. The alternative, therefore, is a level of risk at which a violation would not be disastrous. Any such judgment cannot be purely technical in nature. It must also weigh political considerations, such as the value of setting some first-step inspection machinery in place in order to test the reliability both of the system and of the governments participating in the treaty.

The major obstacle to an across-the-board test-ban agreement so far has been the difficulty in reconciling what each side feels are its minimum national security requirements. Britain and the United States have placed high priority on reliable international detection and inspection machinery; the Soviet Union has given high priority, on military secrecy grounds, to national detection systems.

DEMILITARIZATION AND NEUTRALIZATION

Political agreements to limit or prohibit armaments in particular zones or countries have been attempted several times since the end of World War II, but with more failure than success.

Germany and Japan were demilitarized under occupation supervision immediately after they surrendered. In a little over ten years of cold war, however, both Germanys were integrated into opposing military pacts—the Federal Republic (West Germany) into NATO and the Democratic Republic (Communist East Germany) into the Warsaw Pact. Rearmament followed. A Japanese "self-defense force" has also been established, and the U.S.-Japanese Treaty of 1960 allied the two nations militarily.

The Korean Armistice of 1953 called for a "freeze" on military power in North and South Korea and ultimate withdrawal of foreign troops. In 1957 the UN command in South Korea abrogated the agreement on the grounds that Communist China had been guilty of persistent violations in bringing new weapons into North Korea and that the truce supervision body was denied access to North Korea for purposes of verifying foreign troop movements.

The Austrian State Treaty (1955) "neutralized" that country in the sense that Austria undertook commitments not to ally itself with either military bloc although no limits were placed on its national military establishment. Thus Austria joined ranks with the historical neutrals, Sweden and Switzerland.

Laos, long a battleground of Communist, neutralist and pro-Western forces, was to be neutralized by the 14-power Geneva Agreement of 1962, which called for the withdrawal of all foreign troops (Western and Communist Chinese military advisers and Communist North Vietnamese advisers and troops) under supervision of a Canadian-Indian-Polish Control Commission. The commission, hampered by the requirement of unanimity (a form of *troika*) has not operated success-fully, foreign troops and advisers remain in Laos, the civil war has con-tinued and the neutralist government has been unable to extend effective control over more than a fraction of the national territory. Laos has not been successfully neutralized.

The twelve-nation Antarctica Treaty of 1959, with the United States and Soviet Union as signatories, calls for the permanent non-militarization of that continent and has been cited as a demonstration that such treaties are possible. Antarctica is unique in many respects, however, and the agreement may be more symbolic than precedent-setting.

DISENGAGEMENT

Poland's Foreign Minister Adam Rapacki proposed in 1957 a plan for the denuclearization of four states in Central Europe—the Federal Republic of Germany, the German Democratic Republic, Czechoslo-vakia and Poland. The plan was offered as a prelude to "disengage-ment," or the staged withdrawal of Soviet and Allied troops from direct confrontation in the heart of Europe.

Although the proposal was rejected by the United States and its German ally at the time, the principle of disengagement continues to be discussed. (The principle had been proposed even earlier than 1957, in fact, by British, Irish, U.S. and other Western statesmen, but not in such specific terms as the Rapacki Plan.)

The constructive intent of disengagement (like demilitarization and neutralization) is to remove a sensitive or potentially dangerous zone from the arena of military power competition. A possible by-product of a workable disengagement plan would be the opportunity to experiment with the political and technical machinery required to inspect and control the agreed arms limitations. In addition, disengage-ment has been suggested as a way of reducing the dangers and tensions of direct superpower confrontation in areas such as divided Berlin and the border dividing West and East Germany.

The Western objection to the Rapacki Plan was that it would be militarily unfavorable to NATO. The Federal Republic of Germany, by necessary implication, would withdraw from NATO and NATO would lose its depth in defense. The Rhine rather than the iron curtain would become NATO's eastern frontier. Soviet troops, however, would be required to withdraw a relatively short distance—to the eastern Polish frontier.

Disengagement, whether in Central Europe or elsewhere, may nonetheless have some value in a future arms control agreement or as a step in a universal disarmament agreement. The stumbling block is the difficulty in defining a zone or region where the advantages of denuclearization or a troop pull-back would outweigh any strategic inconveniences or where neither side would be strategically disadvantaged. Soviet proposals in 1963 to denuclearize the Mediterranean would not meet these requirements since only the United States maintains nuclear armaments in the area, notably its Polaris submarine fleet, which is rapidly replacing land-based missiles on the territories of NATO allies.

BROAD-SCALE ARMS REDUCTIONS

The most sweeping arms control proposals are those which call for major reductions in national armaments and force levels, together with some system for verification and inspection. A variety of arms control proposals on this scale have periodically been discussed, within and outside UN channels, since the end of World War II. (These proposals have usually been advanced as "disarmament" plans although, until very recently, none made any specific provisions for the total dismantling of national military forces.)

Discussions of broad-scale arms control have generally bogged down in disputes over phasing, inspection and control.

PHASING.

From the outset, a major obstacle to agreement on the phasing of the arms reduction process was the question of whether a declaratory prohibition on all nuclear weapons should precede any reductions in conventional forces. This was the Soviet view during the pre-1949 period of U.S. atomic monopoly and for some years thereafter. Recently, as Soviet nuclear power grew, Moscow became more amenable to simultaneous reductions in nuclear and conventional forces, across-the-board, in balanced stages. A number of unresolved problems remained, however, in the search for a phasing formula which would take account of the differing strategic requirements of the two sides—Soviet dependence on the numerical superiority of its conventional forces combined with a limited but growing nuclear striking force, all concentrated in a contiguous heartland, and Western dependence on nuclear superiority combined with relatively smaller conventional forces, all dispersed in a global system of foreign alliances and bases.

INSPECTION.

A major stumbling block from the outset was the timing, extent and nature of a system for verifying the arms reduction process and a system of continuing inspection to assure compliance with the arms control agreement. The West insisted on extensive international inspection beginning with the first stage of the arms reduction process. It also insisted on verification of armaments remaining as well as armaments destroyed at each stage of the process. The Soviet Union rejected these proposals as a device for Western espionage. Moscow preferred to limit verification to armaments actually destroyed although it expressed a willingness to accept progressively more thorough inspection as the arms reductions proceeded in stages.

CONTROL.

East and West have also disagreed on the make-up of the machinery for policing or controlling the arms agreement once it is in force. The West would give broad powers to an impartial international control system whereas the Soviet Union would give limited power to an international inspectorate in which it retained a veto.

Since 1960 these same complex and interrelated problems have been dealt with in a somewhat different context—that of general and complete disarmament, a problem you will explore in the next session.

ANOTHER LOOK AT THE TRANSITIONAL PROBLEM

Past negotiations on broad-scale arms control have been unable to surmount two related impasses: (a) how to move through the stages of an arms reduction plan without, at any point, seriously jeopardizing the security of either side and (b) after the final stage has been completed, how to insure international stability—as well as national security—at the reduced levels of competitive national military power.

Put in other terms, the problem has been how to maintain a workable power balance during and after a major tampering with the military forces which make up the contemporary power balance.

In grappling with this challenge, political and technical experts (particularly in the West) have increasingly focused their attention on the security and stability problems that would follow the fulfillment of an extensive arms-reduction plan. The difficulty is not only how to get someplace, but also where you are when you get there.

The challenge of the moment is whether the process can be got under way, whether any momentum can be built up—either at the negotiating table or at the more primitive levels of tacit, unilateral initiatives.

DEMONSTRATION, RATHER THAN NEGOTIATION

There is a school of thought which is firmly convinced that in spite of intermittent conferencing, progress at the negotiating table is highly improbable under existing conditions—either because of the intransigence of one or both sides or because the conflicting views of national security needs on both sides are genuinely irreconcilable. The recommended alternative is action or demonstration, rather than negotiation.

The most radical proposal of this kind is unilateral disarmament. There are a very few who have urged that the United States disarm unilaterally in the hope or expectation that the Russians will accept this gesture in good faith and will follow suit. Some have expressed the belief that, even if the Soviet Union were to use such an opportunity to take over the world, humanity would still be "better Red than dead." The fundamental conviction behind such a view is that war, under present conditions, is unthinkable—or, put another way, that peace under any conditions is preferable to war.

This extreme position is by no means typical of the unilateral approach, however. Indeed, various unilateral initiatives have been taken—and have been reciprocated—in the course of the cold war. Some of these initiatives led to tacit agreements described earlier in this session. Others have simply served immediate strategic or political objectives or have contributed to some superficial "normalization" of relations—evacuation by the U.S. Navy of Republic of China troops from the offshore Tachen Islands in 1955, relinquishment of Soviet control over the Polish military establishment in 1956, reciprocal relaxation of travel restrictions on both sides and various cultural exchange arrangements. More recently the United States revealed it was contemplating cuts in its weapons production—not precisely as a concession but because nuclear stockpiles may be adequate or excessive for foreseeable military requirements. Even so, the decision could have diplomatic value.

What is frequently proposed is the deliberate use of unilateral initiatives as a peace-building strategy. The United States, for example, might initiate a series of modest measures that (a) would not jeopardize U.S. security but (b) might persuade the Soviet Union to follow suit with similar demonstrations of peaceful intent. The challenge facing U.S. policy-makers in such a strategy would be two-fold: (a) How much unilateral initiative is possible without endangering national security? and (b) At what point should an attempt be made to translate a series of initiatives on *peripheral* problems into a serious negotiating effort on the *basic* problem of bringing the military aspect of national power under effective control?

LOOKING AHEAD

The problem of arms control—limited steps or broad-scale measures, unilateral initiatives and tacit agreements or formally negotiated treaties—is as much political as it is technical. Progress in this field depends on the determination of both sides to move toward a more stable and more reliable international system and the willingness of both sides to begin to move in that direction.

SUGGESTED READINGS:

MENDLOVITZ, pp. 557-630.

ADDITIONAL READINGS:

KISSINGER, HENRY A. "Arms Control, Inspection and Surprise Attack." *Foreign Affairs* 38: 557-575 (July, 1960).

OSGOOD, CHARLES EGERTON. "A Case for Graduated Unilateral Disengagement," 16, *Bulletin of the Atomic Scientists* 127 (1960).

WASKOW, ARTHUR I. "The Limits of Defense." *Atlantic Monthly* 209: 80-98 (Feb. 1962).

"Verification and Response in Disarmament Agreements." *Woods Hole Summer Study*. Washington: Institute for Defense Analyses, pp. 47-86. November, 1962.

REFERENCES:

BULL, HEDLEY. *The Control of the Arms Race*. NY: Praeger, 1961.

FRISCH, DAVID H. (ed.). *Arms Reduction: Program and Issues*. NY: Twentieth Century Fund, 1961.

HENKIN, LOUIS (ed.). *Arms Control: Issues for the Public*, published for the American Assembly, Columbia University. Englewood Cliffs, N. J.: Prentice-Hall, 1961.

SCHELLING, THOMAS C., and MORTON H. HALPERIN. *Strategy and Arms Control*. NY: The Twentieth Century Fund, 1961.

Session Seven   QUESTIONS FOR REFLECTION OR DISCUSSION

1. What are the prospects for stabilizing the present military competition?

In view of the tacit restraints which both superpowers have exercised so far in the cold war, how stable do you think the present military competition really is? Do you think it can last for an indefinite period, without serious danger of major thermonuclear war? Why or why not?

What is the value, if any, of tacit agreements on, for example, nondispersal of nuclear weapons technology? on mutual restraint in civil defense? What is the value of the formally negotiated hot-line telecommunications arrangement? of the three-power limited test-ban treaty signed in 1963?

Are there other limited steps which, in your opinion, might reduce the danger of accidental war, relax tensions or build mutual confidence? What are some possible examples?

Do you see any value in unenforced moratoriums or declaratory prohibitions, such as a mutual nonaggression pledge? Any dangers?

2. Would mutual nuclear deterrence be a stable form of arms control?

Review the seven suggested characteristics of a stabilized nuclear deterrence system described on pages 130–131. In your opinion, what are the prospects of achieving each of these conditions by 1970? If all or most of these conditions were achieved by that time, how stable and durable do you think the system would be? What would be its major strengths? Major weaknesses?

Do you think finite deterrence is a bizzare or cynical proposal? or a logical extension of the present system?

Do you think it is likely or unlikely that the United States would accept weapons parity—a more genuine military balance—with the Soviet Union in order to achieve greater stability in the power competition? Why or why not?

3. What is the value of a transitional approach to arms control?

Do you believe there is any point to a peace-building strategy based on successive arms control steps? Is there any point to an arms control measure which does not anticipate some further progress? Why or why not?

What is the transitional value—if any—of each of the following proposals: a verified and inspected ban on all nuclear tests, demilitarization of a particular country or zone, neutralization of a particular country such as Laos, disengagement in Central Europe? Are there also some dangers in such measures? How is it possible to measure the relative risk—benefit versus danger—in each case?

SUMMARY QUESTION:

Can you think of any unilateral initiatives which the United States or the Soviet Union might take now, and which the other side might reciprocate, which would have some transitional benefits?

PROSPECTS FOR GENERAL AND
COMPLETE DISARMAMENT

IN PRINCIPLE, THE UNITED STATES AND THE SOVIET Union—in fact, the entire UN membership—are now committed to the goal of "general and complete disarmament." This is a term that is often used imprecisely and frequently means different things to different individuals and governments.

Since the summer of 1961, however, when the United States and the Soviet Union hammered out a draft statement of mutually acceptable principles governing general and complete disarmament, there has been an "official" UN definition.

General and complete disarmament means, in the long run, the elimination of all national military forces, leaving each nation with nothing more than domestic police or militia. It is a comprehensive and universal term: it applies to all war-making weapons, nuclear and conventional, all types of armed forces and all nations. It calls for elimination of the war-making capacity of every nation on earth.

Furthermore, according to the U.S.-Soviet statement of principles adopted by the UN, general and complete disarmament requires "the establishment of reliable procedures for the peaceful settlement of disputes and effective arrangements for the maintenance of peace in accordance with the principles of the United Nations Charter." These "effective arrangements" specifically include the establishment of a UN peace force. "Arrangements for the use of this force should insure that the United Nations can effectively deter or suppress any threat or use of arms in violation of the purposes and principles of the United Nations."

Yet, in spite of this broad agrement on paper, there has been little or no progress in disarmament negotiations since the principles were adopted. The obstacles to agreement are both technical and political.

There are differing views of what constitute reliable procedures for inspecting and enforcing disarmament and what are effective arrangements for maintaining peace. Perhaps most important, there are very different views of how much independent authority the UN must have and whether it should be effective in "any threat or use of arms" or only in certain kinds of threats.

To understand the difficulties of reaching concrete agreement, it will be helpful to review briefly the major turning-points in postwar negotiations on disarmament and arms control, and then to evaluate the 1962 U.S. and Soviet draft treaties on general and complete disarmament—the drafts which provide the basis for current negotiations.

EARLY ARMS TALKS

Although "disarmament" has been on the agenda of the UN, and of several conferences outside the UN, since 1946, the early negotiations focused largely on technical problems of arms control, rather than on disarmament in the current sense. From 1946 until early 1950 the emphasis was on controlling nuclear energy and nuclear weapons, with very little—and quite separate—attention being given to the problem of regulating non-nuclear or conventional armaments.

By 1950 it was clear that nuclear and non-nuclear problems were inseparably related. The Soviet Union had already (1949) broken the U.S. atomic monopoly and the nuclear arms race was in progress. Under the umbrella of U.S. nuclear superiority, Western Europe was moving (but very slowly) to build up its conventional armed forces as a counter to overwhelming Soviet conventional superiority on the continent of Europe. During the build-up period (which has still not been completed) the West has relied primarily on nuclear power to deter both conventional and nuclear power of the Soviet Union. Obviously, therefore, negotiations to regulate one type of armaments could not ignore the other type.

In 1951 the General Assembly defined the aims of the newly established Disarmament Commission in terms of interrelated arms control measures:

1. Regulation and balanced reduction of all armed forces and armaments—that is, conventional arms reductions with controls.

2. Elimination of all weapons of mass destruction—that is, abolishment of all nuclear weapons.

3. Effective international control of atomic energy.

4. Safeguards—that is, inspection and verification to detect noncompliance with an agreement.

These terms of reference outlined nothing more than a broad-scale arms control arrangement in which nuclear weapons would be prohibited and other weapons and force levels would be scaled down. Not until the following year did the negotiators face some of the implications of comprehensive disarmament.

In 1952 the United States submitted to the UN Disarmament Commission an analysis of "Essential Principles for a Disarmament Program." A key idea was that the purpose of disarmament should be to prevent, not merely to regulate, war. All armaments should be reduced, in other words, to a level which would make war virtually impossible. Moreover, no nation should "be in a position to undertake preparations for war without other States having knowledge of such preparations long before an offending State could start a war."

'ABSOLUTE SAFEGUARDS' VERSUS 'RELATIVE RISKS'

By 1955, as intensive negotiations brought East and West closer together than ever before on technical questions such as phasing of the arms reduction process, a new and serious technical problem emerged and, with it, new political considerations.

It became clear to all concerned that nuclear technology had gone so far—and nuclear armaments had proliferated so rapidly—that a foolproof inspection system had become both technically and politically infeasible. No imaginable inspection system could provide absolute assurances against small caches of nuclear weapons or weapons materials that had been deliberately secreted; any inspection system that came anywhere close to this technical ideal would be so cumbersome and pervasive that it would no doubt be politically intolerable to governments and peoples alike. Disarmament negotiators began to recognize that the earlier goal of "absolute safeguards" would probably have to give way to a concept of "relative risks."

The principle of relative risks is not an unfamiliar one in domestic polity. In a national society operating under law, there are no absolute safeguards against hidden private arsenals or against occasional outbursts of criminal violence. In pragmatic terms, a society cannot "stamp out" all crime even if it is willing to accept total surveillance of all private activity—in short, a police state. Furthermore, if a society values privacy and individual liberty, it tries to strike a tolerable balance between (a) effective law enforcement and (b) noninterference in the normal private pursuits of its citizens. The price of maximum private liberty is the risk of some lawlessness. By placing high risks on socially dangerous crimes, the society is able to deter many crimes while it apprehends and punishes others. By avoiding intrusive and pervasive crime-prevention measures, the society risks some crime but, hopefully, at manageable levels.

The problem is even more acute in the international society, where the task is not law-enforcement among individuals, but peace-enforcement among sovereign nations. Since absolute safeguards are impossible and since it is also undesirable to interfere excessively in the domestic affairs of nations, then the international community must be willing to take some risks. The problem is to balance one risk against the others. This means as much inspection and control as may be necessary to deter or prevent any nation from committing a serious violation that would endanger the security of other nations and the stability of the international system. Yet the inspection and control system should create "a minimum of interference in the internal life of the respective countries."

Put in other terms, nations may have no natural desire to give up the independent military power on which their security has traditionally depended—especially if the disarmament control system seems to have some loopholes in it. Nor is any nation anxious to open up its domestic activities to external scrutiny and regulation. Yet nations may be willing to accept a disarmament plan which balances out these seemingly incompatible needs. The requirements are these: the disarmament inspection and control system must not interfere excessively with domestic affairs, the loopholes for violations must be relatively small, the violations that are possible must not be too dangerous, and, in balance, the risks of the disarmament arrangement must be far less dangerous than the risks of the uncontrolled arms race—both to national security and to international stability.

This principle was apparently understood on all sides but this did not speed agreement on disarmament. On the contrary, as the negotiations wore on, both sides recognized the difficulty of reaching comprehensive agreement on so delicate a balance. The emphasis shifted from comprehensive proposals to first steps and confidence-building measures. The United States, in fact, put a moratorium on all its earlier proposals and refused to discuss any broad-scale plans. Instead U.S. negotiators turned their full attention to limited measures such as "open skies" (mutual aerial inspection to guard against surprise attack), zonal disarmament (reciprocal ground and air inspection of zones in which armaments have been eliminated or drastically reduced) and a nuclear test ban. The briefly hopeful atmosphere of the mid-1955 arms talks, when some observers expected a general treaty might be signed, soon dissipated.

'GENERAL AND COMPLETE DISARMAMENT'

The next major turning point in the arms talks was in 1959 when the Soviet Union called for "general and complete disarmament." Chairman Khrushchev's personal appeal to the Fourteenth General Assembly was followed by a Soviet memorandum which was vague in particulars and sweeping in goals. It called for, among other things, the following measures:

"The disbanding of all armed forces . . . and the prohibition of their re-establishment . . . ;

"The elimination of all . . . types of military equipment;

"The complete prohibition of atomic and hydrogen weapons . . . and the destruction of stockpiles;

"The complete cessation of the manufacture . . . of all types of war missiles, . . . including military space vehicles;

"The prohibition of the production, possession and storage of the means of chemical and bacteriological warfare . . . ;

"The abolition of military bases of all kinds . . . in the territories of foreign States . . . ;

"The cessation of military production . . . ;

"The termination of all military courses and training . . . legislation abolishing military service; . . . abolition of war ministries;
. . . discontinuance of the appropriation of funds for military purposes; . . . prohibition by law of war propaganda . . ." and other
specifics, including the establishment of an international control
organ which would have "all the facilities necessary for the exercise of strict control" over the disarmament program. Disarmament was to be accomplished "within as short a time limit as possible
— within a period of four years."

Although Western governments were highly skeptical of Soviet intentions and labeled the Soviet memorandum "propaganda," the topic
of universal disarmament had unquestionably usurped first place on the
agenda. Indeed, having got wind of Russia's intentions, Britain presented to the UN its own plan for general and complete disarmament
one day ahead of the Soviet presentation.

IMPLICATIONS OF COMPREHENSIVE DISARMAMENT

The subsequent General Assembly debate on general and complete
disarmament acknowledged the radical implications of the proposals. It
was clear to all observers that the elimination of all national armaments
would create unprecedented vacuums in the international system. While
some governments—the Soviet Union in particular—ostensibly saw no
problems in this, the prevailing view was that a disarmed world would
require vastly strengthened legal processes and institutions and, probably,
an international police force with a world monopoly on military power.

In the arms talks which followed, however, very little attention
was paid to the long-term implications of universal disarmament. Russian
negotiators were interested primarily in getting quick agreement to the
principle of total disarmament and adoption of the broad outlines of a
plan to achieve it as rapidly as possible. Western negotiators were still
interested primarily in discussing "first steps" and had not yet worked
out any serious proposals of their own for comprehensive disarmament.
No one was interested, at least initially, in discussing the structure and
problems of a disarmed world. Discussion of disarmament was also
sidetracked, during 1961, first, by prolonged and frustrated negotiations

on a test-ban treaty and later, by Soviet resumption of testing in spite of the tacit moratorium on tests which had been in effect.

In September 1961, in the midst of traded recriminations over resumed testing (U.S. tests followed the Soviet test series), the United States and the Soviet Union reached agreement on the previously described principles to guide negotiations on general and complete disarmament. In the same month President Kennedy addressed the UN, outlining U.S. approaches to general and complete disarmament. In March 1962 the Soviet Union put its proposals in the form of a draft treaty and, a month later, the United States submitted its own draft treaty. These two drafts formally committed both nations to the goal of universal disarmament and provided the basis for subsequent negotiations in the UN Disarmament Committee.

INTENT OF THE DRAFT TREATIES

In many superficial respects the U.S. and Soviet drafts are very similar. Both call for universal and comprehensive nuclear and conventional disarmament, leaving each nation with nothing more than domestic police or militia. (In the Soviet plan, however, the duties of the police would include "safeguarding of the frontiers," a traditional function of national armies.) Both call for inspected disarmament in three stages. (Disarmament would be completed in four years under the Soviet plan and in something over six years—perhaps as long as twelve years—under the U.S. plan.) Both call for the establishment of an International Disarmament Organization (IDO) to supervise the disarming process and both specify that the IDO would operate within the framework of the UN. Both call for a strengthened UN and the establishment of a UN peace force. Both specify various additional measures to inhibit rearmament after the disarming process has been completed.

The differences between the two drafts—and they are significant differences—hinge largely on the question of balancing relative risks. The U.S. plan proposes broad and independent international authority to enforce disarmament and reduce the risk of surreptitious violations; the Soviet draft proposes various political safeguards—including the veto and a *troika* command over the peace force—to reduce the risk of international intervention in the internal affairs of nations, or in the ideological concerns of blocs of nations.

DIVERGENT APPROACHES TO PEACE-ENFORCEMENT

There is a significant divergence between the two drafts in the make-up and political control of the proposed UN peace force.

The Soviet draft provides for the type of peace force originally envisaged by the framers of the UN Charter—stand-by national military units on call to the Security Council under special agreements negotiated according to Article 43. These agreements would be concluded before the disarmament treaty came into effect. In the third and final stage of the disarming process, when all national military forces would have been reduced to the level of domestic police or militia, the stand-by units available to the Security Council would be police units, strictly speaking, rather than military units. Apart from this semantic distinction, the mechanism for peace-enforcement would be the same both during the disarming process and after disarmament had been completed. It would consist of national units which the Security Council could mobilize in a crisis *if the five permanent members of the Council agreed unanimously to do so.* The veto, in other words, would become a permanent fixture of a disarmed world. In addition, the peace forces mobilized by the Security Council would be commanded by a *troika* representing the three blocs of nations in the Soviet world-view: Communist, capitalist and neutralist. Any peace-enforcement move or strategy would require unanimity among these three coequal commanders.

The U.S. draft suggests "examination of the feasibility of concluding promptly the agreements envisaged in Article 43." It also anticipates that, at the end of the third and final disarming stage, the remaining national police and militia would be of sufficient size "that they would be capable of providing agreed manpower" for the UN peace force. Otherwise the U.S. plan is open about the make-up of the proposed UN peace force—whether it would be made up exclusively of stand-by national units, whether it might include "fire brigade" units such as those being set up by the Nordic nations, or whether it might even include professional units under permanent UN command. None of these possibilities is excluded in the U.S. draft treaty provisions calling for an examination of past UN peace force experiences and then for "Conclusion of an agreement for the establishment of a United Nations Peace Force in Stage II [of the disarming process], including definitions of its purpose, mission, composition and strength, disposition, command and control, training, logistical support, financing, equipment and armaments."

The U.S. draft is explicit on certain points, however. Detailed arrangements for setting up the peace force would be completed in the first stage. The peace force would be set up in the second stage. It would be progressively strengthened during Stage II until, in the third stage, it would have "sufficient armed forces and armaments so that no state could challenge it."

SUPERVISION OF DISARMAMENT

Superficially (as mentioned earlier) the two drafts propose a similar institutional framework for supervising disarmament. Both plans call for a new agency—the IDO—which in many respects would parallel the UN. The principal organs of the IDO would include a General Conference (or simply Conference in the Soviet version) with functions resembling those of the UN General Assembly, and a Control Council resembling the UN Security Council. The General Conference would consist of all nations signing the disarmament treaty and would have wide latitude for discussion and recommendation on matters related to disarmament. Under neither plan would the General Conference have any legislative powers although, in the U.S. plan, it would have the power of "deciding" on matters referred to it by the Control Council.

The Control Council, under both plans, would consist of the major powers as permanent members plus other nations elected on a rotating basis. There is no mention of a veto in the Control Council in either the U.S. or Soviet plan although the Soviet draft specifies that the Council's membership reflect "proper representation of the three groups of states existing in the world."

Under both plans the General Conference would elect the nonpermanent members of the Control Council, approve the IDO budget recommended by the Control Council, and make any recommendations or proposals it wished to the Council. The Control Council, under both plans, would supervise disarmament control operations.

The two plans differ in their proposals for the IDO staff, which would roughly parallel the UN Secretariat in functions. The U.S. draft calls for an impartial Administrator to be appointed by the General Conference on recommendation of the Control Council, in a manner resembling the UN's system for appointing its Secretary-General. The IDO Administrator would be chief executive officer and would administer the verification and inspection system which the IDO would establish throughout the world. In these activities he would be supervised by the Control Council. He would also prepare the IDO budget for submission to the Control Council and General Conference and would report to the Control Council on the progress of the disarming process.

Under the Soviet plan the staff of the IDO would be recruited by the Control Council "on an international basis, so as to ensure that the three principal groups of states existing in the world are adequately represented." The plan makes no mention of an executive officer nor, indeed, does it assign any executive functions to the staff. Executive powers of the IDO, such as they are, would be confined to the Control Council, where the five major powers and the three power blocs would be represented (although apparently without formal veto).

The most important difference in the two proposals is not, however, in the structure of the IDO. (The IDO would have relatively narrow independent power, anyway, under either plan.) The key difference is in the proposed relationship between the IDO and the UN.

POLITICAL CONTROL OVER PEACE-ENFORCEMENT

Under both plans, political control over disarmament and peace-enforcement would rest with the UN, although the U.S. draft is vague in its description of the procedures. Under the Soviet plan this political control would rest exclusively with the UN Security Council: "All questions related to the assurance of international peace and security, which may arise in the course of the implementation of the [disarmament] treaty, including preventive and enforcement measures, shall be decided on by the Security Council in conformity with its powers under the United Nations Charter."

It is no oversimplification to say that the Soviet draft treaty for general and complete disarmament simply reinforces Moscow's well publicized attitude toward the UN. It restates Soviet insistence on a strict construction of the UN Charter. The "primary responsibility" of the Security Council for the maintenance of international peace and security is reaffirmed and broadened to include the area of enforcing disarmament. All peace-force matters, including financing, would rest exclusively with the Security Council, subject to great-power unanimity. The Secretary-General would have no initiatives in the peace-enforcement area since only the Security Council could mobilize the force. Moreover, all command responsibilities over the peace force would be lodged with a *troika* body under the Council's political control.

Nor is it an oversimplification to say that the U.S. draft treaty for general and complete disarmament expresses (however vaguely) well known U.S. attitudes toward peace-enforcement. No restraints are suggested on the peace-enforcement initiatives of either the General Assembly or the Secretary-General. Indeed, the U.S. draft calls for "measures to improve the capability of the United Nations to maintain international peace and security." It also calls for codification and extension of international law, measures to eliminate the risks of indirect aggression and subversion, and a strengthening of processes for the peaceful resolution of both legal and political disputes. Finally, to insure that international authorities will be able to rely on the legal use of force to prevent the illegal use of force, the U.S. draft calls for progressive strengthening of the UN peace force until it will be so powerful no nation will be able to defy it.

Washington's view of a disarmed world (according to its 1962 draft treaty) is one in which the present competitive power system, based on national armaments, is replaced by strengthened international law and institutions, backed by adequate international force that is unhampered by veto. Washington would strengthen the UN by extending its independent power of action.

Moscow's view of a disarmed world (according to its draft) is one in which disarmament alone insures peace and the UN is specifically prohibited from intervening in any conflict or dispute in which the interests of any one of the five great powers, or any of the three power blocs, might be jeopardized by that intervention. Moscow would strengthen the UN by returning to the Charter-framers' original concepts of Security Council primacy and great-power unanimity.

CAN THE DIFFERENCES BE RECONCILED?

On many of the key technical issues, the two drafts do not appear to be far apart. Both agree on the need for "balanced reductions" in armaments and force levels to insure that neither side will be militarily disadvantaged at any stage of the disarming process. Both agree that there should be no more inspection, at any stage of the disarming process, than that stage calls for—that is, there should be only as much interference in domestic activities of each nation as all nations require, and are willing to accept reciprocally, for their own security. Both also agree that inspection and control should be unhampered and unrestricted once the disarming process is completed.

It is of course possible that serious negotiations would reveal deeper cleavages on technical questions than the language of the two drafts suggests. The serious divisions appear to be political, rather than technical, however.

The two divergent views of the UN, which have been discussed in previous sessions and which are clearly revealed in the two treaty drafts, represent wholly different attitudes toward international law, national sovereignty, and the potential capacity of international institutions to serve as impartial regulators of international relations.

The important common ground, apparently, is that steps must be taken to reduce the danger of major nuclear war — and that the way to do this is to eliminate national war-making power under some form of mutually acceptable international control. Both sides also agree that the UN should have some enforcement authority and police power in any such arrangement.

The core difficulty is in the way this power should be used — the degree of international intervention in affairs within and between states that is tolerable to each side. In a disarmed world, for example, should the UN be allowed to call up the peace force in order to put down a civil uprising which threatens international peace and in which the opposing forces are pro-Communist and pro-Western? If so, on which side should the UN intervene? In case of an uprising based on minority self-determination or on Irredentism — the Kurds, Pathans, Tibetans, Palestinian Arabs, Prussians or some other aggrieved group — what role should the international peace-keeping agency play, if any? Could the issue be resolved impartially by international legal processes? Could it be resolved justly by international armed intervention? Finally, unless the peace-keeping authority has some clear and legal power in disputes such as these, would there be any sure way of preventing the conflict from spreading — either with the primitive arms available to nations in a disarmed world or through sudden rearmament of one or more nations?

These are, of course, unanswered questions in both treaty drafts. Yet they are crucial questions if divergent attitudes toward comprehensive disarmament are to be reconciled.

IS GENERAL AND COMPLETE DISARMAMENT FEASIBLE?

It is one thing to inquire whether the two draft treaties — or, more fundamentally, the divergent positions of East and West — can be reconciled through negotiation and recognition of common interest. It is quite another to inquire whether either draft, or any conceivable compromise between the two, would provide an adequate framework for general and complete disarmament. Under any comparable plan, in other words, would universal disarmament even be feasible? A great many experts think not.

The major criticism of both drafts is that neither goes far enough in providing adequate safeguards (a) for the legitimate differences among nations and peoples with different backgrounds, conditions, needs and problems; (b) for the universal interest of all nations and peoples in a warless world; and (c) for peaceful change, and resolution of disputes, under law.

To pinpoint this criticism it will be helpful to look once again at the Clark-Sohn model of a world peace system. While this model is, in itself, open to criticism it nonetheless suggests in graphic terms the broad framework and principal elements of an international system in which general and complete disarmament might be acceptable to most peoples.

CLARK-SOHN TREATY PROPOSALS

The original Clark-Sohn proposals were set forth in the form of proposed revisions to the UN Charter. In May 1962, in the wake of publication of the Soviet and U.S. draft treaties, these two experts revamped their proposals in the form of a summary of a draft treaty which could be negotiated without any revisions to the UN Charter. The basic provisions were unchanged. The only change was in format. The controlling idea in both cases is that general and complete disarmament is impractical unless the following conditions are met:

1. Some measure of enforceable world law is brought into effect, backed by a world monopoly on military power, in order to prohibit, deter and punish the use of force by nations or groups of nations.

2. Adequate procedures are developed for the peaceful resolution of international disputes, under law, including a world judicial and conciliation system.

3. Adequate procedures are developed to channel world capital and technology into a massive effort to reduce economic inequality among nations and thus remove many of the inequities which lead to international tension and dispute.

To achieve these conditions, Clark and Sohn would establish — in place of the IDO or International Disarmament Organization — a World Disarmament and World Development Organization which would operate within the UN framework but would be largely self-sufficient in the areas of enforcing disarmament, providing new channels for the peaceful resolution of disputes, and providing for a major world development effort. The new organization would supplement existing UN machinery but would not be dependent in powers or finances on the UN.

MAIN FEATURES OF THE PROPOSED ORGANIZATION

The foundation of the Clark-Sohn proposal is comprehensive and universal disarmament, with adequate inspection and enforcement machinery, plus world legislative, executive and judicial institutions, a world development agency and an adequate and reliable revenue system. These essential elements may be summarized as follows:

DISARMAMENT PLAN.

The disarming process would involve annual reductions in military strength of 10 percent, over a 10-year period, under international inspection. A portion of the armaments released from national military establishments (including a small nuclear armory) would be turned over to a UN peace force each year until the peace force reached full strength. UN nuclear stockpiles would be held in reserve in case some nation brought similar weapons out of hiding. All other armaments would be destroyed, except for small arms needed for internal police duties.

PEACE FORCE.

At the end of the disarming period the proposed peace force would have an effective strength of 200,000 to 400,000 men, backed by a reserve of 300,000 to 600,000. This UN force would be the only military force remaining in a disarmed world. It would be made up, not of stand-by units in the respective national militia, but of full-time indi· vidual volunteers. It would be a professional force, well paid, strongly armed and highly mobile. It would be under political control of civilian authorities and could go into action "only in carefully defined circumstances where clearly necessary to prevent or suppress international violence."

WORLD LEGISLATIVE AUTHORITY.

The proposed agency would include a General Conference, representative of all member nations—a universal body including the governments of divided nations and other powers, even non-self-governing territories, now outside the UN. Instead of one vote per nation, membership and voting in the General Conference would be based on population (a maximum of thirty and a minimum of one representative per nation). Furthermore, the representatives would vote as individuals rather than as governmental delegates. Originally they would be appointed by national legislatures; ultimately they would be chosen by popular vote in their respective countries. This representative world body would have "primary and general responsibility" for maintaining peace and international security. Its powers would include adoption and assessment of the annual budget for the World Disarmament and World Development Organization, fixing the strength of the UN peace force and adopting its regulations, enactment of penalties for violations of the disarmament treaty, supervision of the World Development Authority, and election of an Executive Council.

WORLD EXECUTIVE AUTHORITY.

An Executive Council would be chosen by (and could be dismissed by) the General Conference. The Council would be responsible to the General Conference and would serve as its agent — a kind of cabinet — in carrying out executive responsibilities under the disarmament treaty and enforcing regulations adopted by the General Conference. The Executive Council would be made up of 17 members, elected from the membership of the General Conference. The four most populous nations would be permanently represented on the Council (China, India, the Soviet Union and United States). The other thirteen members would be selected according to a formula insuring adequate representation for other populous nations and the smaller nations. There would be no veto but the voting system would insure that all important decisions reflected "a strong preponderance of world opinion."

JUDICIAL AND CONCILIATION SYSTEM.

The Clark-Sohn treaty provides for (a) compulsory submission to the International Court of Justice of all international disputes which might endanger the peace and which are subject to judicial decision on the basis of established legal principles and (b) compulsory reference to a World Equity Tribunal (which the treaty would create) of all dangerous international disputes not of a legal nature. In the case of all legal disputes, failure to comply would involve sanctions including, in extreme cases, action by the UN peace force. In the case of disputes referred to the World Equity Tribunal, noncompliance would be subject to review by the General Conference, which could require compliance under pain of sanctions, including action by the peace force. A World Conciliation Board would be available in cases where diplomacy had failed but a settlement might still be negotiated. A system of UN Regional Courts would also be established, with clearly defined functions under the treaty.

WORLD DEVELOPMENT AGENCY.

A World Development Authority would be set up, with a well defined program and adequate budget to speed world economic development and to close as rapidly as possible the gap between "have" and "have-not" nations.

WORLD REVENUE SYSTEM.

The General Conference would be empowered to adopt an annual budget for the whole disarmament and development system, not to exceed 3 percent of the estimated gross world product (value of all goods and services produced in the world in a year). The budget would be apportioned among the membership on the principle of ability to pay. The revenues would be collected by member governments in the form of certain earmarked taxes and would be paid directly into the treasury of the World Disarmament and World Development Organization.

Relations between the new agency and the UN would be carefully stipulated in the treaty. The UN would continue to have the power, under its Charter, to take the initiative in maintaining or restoring international peace — either through the Security Council under Chapter VII of the Charter or through the General Assembly under the Uniting for Peace principle. In such cases the World Disarmament and Development Organization would be bound to support the UN effort. Should the General Conference take a peace-enforcement initiative under its own powers, the UN would not be authorized to revoke or modify the action except by a special and large majority of the General Assembly. The veto, in other words, would not be able to frustrate peace-enforcement in a disarmed world.

LOOKING AHEAD

The prospects for general and complete disarmament will be determined by two vital factors: (a) whether the plan is indeed workable — that is, whether it provides the safeguards to national interests and to international stability that offer some promise of a viable international system, and (b) whether the plan is acceptable — that is, whether it provides enough inducements and opportunities, as well as safeguards, to persuade different nations and peoples that the risks of universal disarmament are far less than the risks of a continuing uncontrolled arms race, and that the prospects for man and his aspirations will be improved in a disarmed world under law.

SUGGESTED READINGS:

MENDLOVITZ, pp. 648-735.
CLARK AND SOHN, pp. 206-213.

ADDITIONAL READINGS:

BLOOMFIELD, LINCOLN P. "Arms Control and World Government."
World Politics 14: 633-645 (July, 1962).

FISHER, ROGER D. "Enforcement of Disarmament: The Problem of
the Response." *Proc. Am. Soc. Int. L.* 56: 1-18 (1962).

McCLOY, JOHN J. "Balance Sheet on Disarmament." *Foreign Affairs*
40: 339-359, (Apr. 1962).

WASKOW, ARTHUR I. *Quis Custodiet? Controlling the Police in a Disarmed World.* Washington: Peace Research Institute, April, 1963.

REFERENCES:

BARNET, RICHARD J. *Who Wants Disarmament?* Boston: Beacon Press,
1960.

WADSWORTH, JAMES J. *The Price of Peace.* NY: Praeger, 1962.

WARBURG, JAMES P. *Disarmament: The Challenge of the Sixties.* NY:
Doubleday, 1961.

Session Eight   QUESTIONS FOR REFLECTION OR
DISCUSSION

*1. What kind of international system would the Soviet draft treaty on
general and complete disarmament create?*

How would the *fact* of general and complete disarmament affect
world politics?

Would it in fact be general and complete disarmament if nations
retained sufficiently powerful militia to "safeguard the frontiers"?

In the absence of a strong international police force, how would
small nations (with relatively small militia) be secure against large nations (with relatively large militia)?

Would the Soviet draft treaty provide any new restraints on the effective power of the major nations — Britain, China, France, the Soviet Union or the United States? On other relatively strong nations — Brazil, India, Indonesia, or the United Arab Republic?

Under the Soviet disarmament system, would the UN be able to deal effectively with the following hypothetical crises:

a. An invasion of Israel by U.A.R.-equipped and supported Palestinian Arab refugees, followed by a general attack on Israel by all its Arab neighbors — using only the militia and armaments permitted under the disarmament treaty?

b. An uprising by the nonwhites of the Republic of South Africa and Southwest Africa against the white government, followed by an invasion of these areas by nonwhite peoples of tropical Africa, using only the small arms permitted under the disarmament treaty?

c. An organized and massive movement of Chinese civilian population into (a) India's unpopulated border highlands or (b) the Soviet Union's sparsely populated border regions?

d. A mob movement (strikes, demonstrations and terror) in a Latin American country such as Brazil, in which the mob is led by local Communists but financed by the Soviet Union and where the objective is to subvert a government supported and partially financed by the United States? (Or a situation in which the roles are reversed, perhaps in Communist East Germany or Poland)?

2. *Does the U.S. draft treaty on general and complete disarmament offer better safeguards for international peace and security?*

Review the four hypothetical crises described in the previous question. In each case, would the U.S. disarmament plan (insofar as it is spelled out) provide the machinery for more effective handling of the situation by a world authority? If so, in what specific ways?

In what ways would the U.S. disarmament plan probably be inadequate in these four cases, or in any one of them? Is this inadequacy of fundamental importance?

SUMMARY QUESTION:

Drawing on the three disarmament proposals — Soviet, U.S. and Clark-Sohn — and on any ideas of your own, what do you think are the essential elements of an effective and acceptable plan for general and complete disarmament? Try drawing up a list of *minimum essential* provisions, institutions and safeguards.

PROBLEMS AND OPPORTUNITIES

OF A DISARMED WORLD

THE WORLD IS NOW SPENDING (ACCORDING TO A 1962 UN estimate) about $120 billion a year to keep 20 million men under arms and perhaps another 30 million employed in defense and defense-related industries. Between 8 and 9 percent of all the goods and services produced in the world are related to military purposes —a value equal to annual world exports of all commodities, or to two-thirds the combined national income of the developing nations.

Beyond any doubt, conversion from an armed to a disarmed world economy would create profound global problems and opportunities in the adjustment, conversion, relocation and reallocation of resources — including human resources. Furthermore, the impact would be much sharper on certain countries, regions, communities, industries and pro- fessions. (Seven nations, for example, account for about 85 percent of the world military outlay: United States, Soviet Union, Communist China, Britain, Canada, France and the Federal Republic of Germany.)

In spite of the obvious magnitude of the problem, relatively little public attention has been devoted to it. Two important official studies have been issued — one by the UN Department of Economic and Social Affairs, in response to a General Assembly resolution requesting such a study, and one by the U.S. Arms Control and Disarmament Agency. (Both superpowers concurred in the UN report.) A handful of private scholars have also conducted their own studies and issued various find- ings and recommendations. Private industries and local communities — which would be most seriously affected by comprehensive disarmament — have paid almost no attention to the problem.

The published official and private studies differ somewhat in their emphasis, their sense of urgency and their specific recommendations.

There is a fair consensus, however, on the following general conclusions:

1. General and complete disarmament (as distinguished from an arms reduction program that would leave nations with significant military capabilities) would transform the economies of some nations, and regions within nations, and would probably alter the patterns of trade and investment throughout the world economy.

2. The transformations are manageable — by individual nations, if there is adequate foresight and planning, and by the world economy, if there is adequate international planning and co-operation.

3. Conversion to a world peace economy would open up unprecedented opportunities for the economic and social advancement of all nations and peoples; however, without study, planning and cooperation, the negative effects of disarmament could be widespread, prolonged, wasteful and painful.

This session will review the major conversion and adjustment problems, for both the industrialized and the developing nations and for the world economy as a whole. It will also explore some of the economic, social and political effects of comprehensive and universal disarmament — the opportunities and hazards of living in a disarmed world.

CONVERTING AN INDUSTRIALIZED NATIONAL ECONOMY

In the broadest and simplest terms, the job of converting a national economy from an armed to a disarmed state (especially a highly industrialized and heavily armed economy) involves four interrelated steps:

ABSORPTION OF MILITARY MANPOWER.

Personnel released from the armed forces will need to find other, gainful employment. Some would no doubt be retained in the national police or militia. Others, depending on the nature of the disarmament agreement, might be transferred to an international peace force. Under any comprehensive disarmament plan, however, the vast majority of the personnel now in various national uniforms would have to be absorbed by the civilian economies of these nations.

ABSORPTION OF DEFENSE-INDUSTRY MANPOWER.

Under comprehensive disarmament, only a very small proportion of those now employed in armament industries (about 2.5 million people in the United States) would remain in that business — specifically, those manufacturing light armaments for domestic police or militia and any who might be required to manufacture heavier weapons for an international peace force. In some defense and defense-related industries — aircraft, vehicles, electronics, space exploration, etc. — some workers would no doubt be shifted to purely civilian manufacturing in the same or similar fields. A full-scale civilian space program, for example, would employ many of the resources now working on military space programs. A large percentage of all those now working in the defense sector, however, would have to transfer to entirely different jobs in the civilian sector of each national economy.

INDUSTRIAL CONVERSION.

Most existing defense plants, and a high proportion of defense-related manufacturing, would become obsolete. Enormous public and private investments in land, plant and technology would have to be reallocated somehow. Highly specialized managerial and professional skills would become surplus — including a significant part of the current investment in research in many industrialized nations. (About half the U.S. research and development effort is defense-related.) These resources would need to be converted to civilian use.

OVER-ALL STABILIZATION AND ECONOMIC EXPANSION.

Finally, the conversion to disarmament would take place within the context of other, "normal" economic changes in each country — normal population growth, normal expansion of the labor force, on-going economic adjustment problems such as surpluses in some work skills and shortages in others, and persisting pockets of chronic unemployment or underemployment — all characteristics of many industrialized societies. Disarmament conversion would seriously aggravate some of these conditions and would create wholly new problems of similar gravity. It would be necessary, therefore, for the entire national economy to accelerate its growth in the production and consumption of both goods and services, during and after the conversion process. The rate of economic growth should be rapid enough, not only to cope with normal growth and adjustment, but also to absorb the impact of disarmament conversion with a minimum of human hardship and economic waste.

MANPOWER PROBLEMS IN INDUSTRIALIZED NATIONS

In any expanding industrialized society there is a normal transfer of manpower between jobs, between localities and between sectors of the economy. These transfers are generally from lower skill to higher skill jobs, from stagnant or slow growing to faster growing industries, from rural to urban labor markets, from stagnant or slow growing local economies to rapidly expanding localities, from agriculture, mining and other traditional sectors to industrialized sectors of the economy. The rates and patterns of transfer vary greatly, of course, from one nation to another.

(In the Soviet Union a major manpower problem is the high proportion of the total labor force — perhaps 50 percent — remaining in agriculture in spite of shortages of workers for relatively more skilled manufacturing and service jobs. In the United States, where the application of farm technology began much earlier and has proceeded very rapidly, only about 7 percent of the total labor force is in agriculture, and the farms supply a steady stream of workers for nonfarm jobs: 7.25 million U.S. farm families moved into the nonfarm sector between 1950 and 1958.)

IMPLICATIONS OF MANPOWER SHIFTS

These shifts take place because of the demands and opportunities of national economic expansion. New investment and technological advances reduce the demand for some jobs and create new jobs which usually require higher skills. New techniques — and domestic or foreign competition — require higher investments in the modernization of plants and methods. Labor-intensive jobs such as agriculture, mining and hand assembly are replaced by more productive and efficient and therefore cheaper machinery. Whole industries increase their output and lower their unit costs by employing fewer (but more skilled and higher paid) workers in automated plants. Workers with the capacity and opportunity to do so move up the scale by upgrading their own skills.

In the process, the "profile" of the national labor force changes. The number of skilled production and service jobs (and the number of skilled workers) increases; the number of unskilled jobs either declines or fails to increase. Obsolete jobs and skills are gradually weeded out of the economy. Workers unable or unwilling to adapt to this changing job-market profile become unemployed or underemployed.

This pattern is particularly obvious in the market economies of Western industrialized nations and Japan. It is also relevant in many respects, however, to centrally planned economies such as the Soviet Union and the industrialized nations of Eastern Europe, although there is a difference in the way the changes are managed. In a centrally planned economy the setting of priorities on certain skills, the upgrading of workers through training, and the transfer of labor from one job or locality to another are generally pursued as matters of public policy under state control. In a market economy these shifts and changes are, to a much greater degree, autonomous. Individuals normally decide for themselves whether to study for or pursue better or different jobs and whether to leave one industry or locality for another. Similarly, capitalists and entrepreneurs normally decide for themselves whether to enter new investment and production fields. The market itself, of course, provides incentives and inducements which influence these decisions and, at times, the society influences individual decision-making as a matter of conscious public policy.

This distinction obviously has some bearing on the way each type of economic system would manage its disarmament conversion problems. In a more fundamental sense, however, both types of economic systems face somewhat similar long-range problems. In any expanding industrial society the growth in job opportunities is taking place primarily at the middle and higher skill levels — engineers and designers, teachers and doctors, managers and administrators, technicians and specialists, foremen and supervisors, machine-operators and repairmen, etc. At the lower skill levels, especially manual and semiskilled labor, job opportunities tend to remain stagnant or actually decline.

In the expanding sectors of the job market the manpower problem is to promote or transfer already qualified individuals or to train others fast enough. In the stagnant or declining sectors, the manpower problem is what to do with the inadequately trained (such as high school dropouts) and untrainable workers whose skills are obsolete or in low demand

and who therefore constitute a surplus in the labor market. This second and more difficult problem is, for example, an important factor in recent (and apparently chronic) high unemployment rates in some parts of the United States and among educationally disadvantaged minorities.

Conversion to disarmament, on top of these already difficult problems, would thus have two serious effects:

RELEASE OF LOW-SKILL LABOR.

A significant proportion of those released from military or defense-related activities — particularly the lower ranks and combat personnel in the armed forces — would be relatively unskilled labor in a civilian sense. Even though modern military forces are far more highly trained than those of half a generation ago, a great many of these skills have little or no applicability to the civilian economy. Thus disarmament would intensify the already grave problem of those who are unemployable unless and until they acquire skills that are in demand.

RELEASE OF MIDDLE AND HIGH SKILL WORKERS AND PROFESSIONALS.

In addition, a large proportion of the highly skilled professionals, technicians and operators released from military service and defense industries would also have difficulty in transferring their skills to civilian pursuits. The costly quality controls typical of defense manufacturing, for example, have very little use in consumer manufacturing — whether in a competitive market economy or a centrally planned economy. The nature and discipline of much defense research is equally foreign to peacetime industry. Even the manager of a U.S. or British defense industry, used to dealing with only one huge contractor, his government, might be expected to encounter difficulties in trying to adapt to competitive marketing and merchandising and the scramble for a share of national and world markets.

To recapitulate, disarmament conversion in a highly industrialized and heavily armed economy would aggravate some already serious manpower problems at the lower ends of the economic scale and would create wholly new problems at the middle and upper ends of the scale.

PROBLEMS OF CONVERTING INDUSTRIES

It is important to recognize that disarmament conversion in the

1960's or 1970's would differ in important ways from the admittedly large-scale arms cutbacks which followed World War II and the Korean War. In the earlier two cases, private industry's main challenge was either to rebuild (in the war-devastated areas) or to reconvert to civilian manufacturing (in those industrialized areas untouched by war). Industries producing defense supplies when both wars ended were, with some important exceptions, peacetime industries that had temporarily diverted part or all of their production to war purposes, especially in Western industrialized nations. With war over, these industries rebuilt or reconverted to their normal pursuits and quickly began to meet pent-up consumer and other peacetime demands.

However, the military arts have progressed enormously since the end of the Korean war, and defense requirements have become infinitely more sophisticated — quantity production of highly refined fissionable materials, development and production of long-range and other missiles and space craft, perfecting of a wide range of atomic hardware, miniaturization of electronic guidance and other equipment, development of small tactical nuclear weapons, development of immensely elaborate and specialized warning and communications systems, perfecting of special alloys for jet engines and space craft, development of specialized military vehicles such as vertical take-off and orbital airplanes and nuclear submarines.

These defense needs are not being met by converted peacetime industries, but by industries which, for the most part, have never or only marginally been in nondefense work, and many of which have been in existence for a very few years. A number of the aircraft industries in the United States, for example, have set up wholly new subsidiaries to handle major defense contracts or have subcontracted to new companies created solely for defense manufacturing. Other industries which have always been in defense work have mushroomed under government contracts. Disarmament for these and similar industries will mean conversion, rather than reconversion. And, for obvious reasons of overspecialization, disarmament conversion for many of these companies will mean destruction of some capital assets and liquidation of others, depreciation of outstanding stock and dispersal of personnel to find new jobs on their own.

GEOGRAPHICAL CONCENTRATION OF DEFENSE INDUSTRIES

There is another and perhaps more serious problem for countries like the United States and Canada, where defense industries have sometimes been deliberately located in localities or regions which would otherwise be industrially poor and where, in any event, major defense complexes have tended to concentrate in a few regions of the country.

For example in the United States, employment in major defense industries constitutes a significant percentage of total manufacturing employment in the following states (April 1960): Kansas, 30.2 percent; Washington, 28.6 percent; New Mexico, 23.8 percent; California, 23.3 percent; Connecticut, 21.1 percent; Arizona, 20.6 percent; Utah, 20.4 percent; Colorado, 17.8 percent; Florida, 14.1 percent. Defense Department payrolls (military pay and allowances and civilian wages and salaries) constitute a high proportion of personal income in the following states: Alaska, 26.5 percent; Hawaii, 18.2 percent; Virginia, 10.2 percent. Disarmament, industrial conversion and military demobilization would obviously have a heavy economic and social impact on these states.

Similarly, the highly specialized aerospace-nucleonic-electronic defense complex is geographically concentrated in parts of Britain and the United States (but probably less so in the Soviet Union). In the United States, for example, this concentration is largely in the Boston-Cambridge, Berkeley-Palo Alto, Pasadena-Los Angeles areas (all major university centers) and in a few other localities such as Houston, Huntsville and Cape Canaveral. To the extent that these complexes are dismantled under disarmament, the surrounding communities—including the academic communities—will be deprived of a considerable share of their present preoccupations and incomes.

In short, in those areas where defense industries or installations provide either important props or the mainstay of the local economy, disarmament conversion may hit hard.

OVER-ALL ADJUSTMENT OF INDUSTRIALIZED ECONOMIES

As suggested by the problems reviewed so far, disarmament conversion in a highly industrialized and heavily armed nation such as the United States, Soviet Union, Britain, Canada, France and the Federal Republic of Germany, would probably involve major structural changes in the whole economy and serious adjustment problems in certain sectors and localities of each society. The dimensions of conversion would be greater in the United States and the Soviet Union, which carry the main armaments burden in the world today, and in some respects they might be greatest in the Soviet Union, whose military expenditures are nearly as large as those of the United States, but whose total economy is only about half of the size of the U.S. economy.

Time factors in the disarming process would certainly be important. Under the Soviet draft proposals for general and complete disarmament, for example, the entire process would have to be completed in four years. A very few Western analysts favor an even shorter conversion period—in spite of economic and social adjustment problems—for political and psychological reasons. They would like the disarmament schedule to move so fast that it might build up momentum to insure against any reversal of the disarming process. Most Western analysts would prefer a longer conversion period to permit reasonable adjustment planning and "cushioning." The U.S. draft proposal calls for two three-year stages followed by a third stage of unspecified duration. Clark and Sohn have suggested a ten or twelve year disarming schedule which could be accelerated en route.

COSTS OF DISARMAMENT

Another important variable is the cost of disarmament institutions—installation and maintenance of the inspection system, maintenance of an international peace force, and operation of any related administrative, judicial, consultative, legislative and/or executive bodies that might be strengthened or created in order to enforce disarmament and provide peaceful alternatives for the resolution of disputes. Some authorities have estimated, for example, that an across-the-board test-ban inspection system (including a ban on underground as well as above-ground tests) might require a $1.7 billion capital outlay. An extensive inspection system for comprehensive disarmament—including inspection teams for factories, military installations and sea, air, road and rail traffic centers —would require even larger initial outlays and maintenance budgets. The Clark-Sohn peace system proposal would cost, in the round, about $36 billion a year—about $9 billion for the UN peace force, a suggested $25 billion for the World Development Authority, and about $2 billion for a strengthened UN system (or World Disarmament and World Development Organization in conjunction with the UN). This would represent about a third of the present annual world outlay for military purposes.

Obviously a comprehensive world peace authority such as Clark and Sohn propose, with its relatively high manpower and budgetary requirements, would help cushion the transition to disarmament by immediately rechanneling substantial human and capital resources into international development programs and peace-force functions. Other authorities question the capacity of the developing nations to make efficient use of as much as $25 billion annually in development funds and some authorities question the $9 billion proposed annual outlay for a UN peace force. Nonetheless, the fact remains that *national* economic adjustments to disarmament would be eased to some extent if *international* cooperative efforts provided opportunities and demands for the constructive employment of otherwise surplus economic resources.

International commitments can absorb only part of the resources which disarmament would render surplus, however. The main challenges to each national economy would be to maintain aggregate national demand at high enough levels to cope with both normal economic adjustments and the special adjustment problems which disarmament will pose—and to make adequate and timely investment in people (through education, training, relocation and other public and private services) and in capital expansion (through investment, tax, trade and other private and public policies) to insure minimum hardship and waste and maximum social benefit.

National growth and adjustment programs of this magnitude will certainly require advance study, broad public and private understanding, and (for some countries) more intensive cooperation between private interests and government (national and local) than may be traditional.

QUALITATIVE ECONOMIC FACTORS

There is another dimension to the disarmament conversion problem which is wholly positive in its implications. This has to do with the relative utility—in economic terms—of investments in military production versus investments in peaceful production. Although the problem has only recently been subjected to intensive analysis, there is increasing recognition that investment in armaments produces far less benefit to an industrialized economy than other types of investment.

This is not to deny the "fallout" benefits from defense research and development—faster and more efficient commercial aircraft, new medical discoveries, commercial application of advances in military electronics and communications, contributions to basic knowledge and human adventure derived from military space programs, the stimulation to employment and trade which defense jobs and wages provide, etc. In economic terms, however, military investments are marginal in a very important sense. The main purpose of the defense sector of an industrialized national economy is not economic utility—it is, rather, to create and maintain vast organized resources which (hopefully) will never be used. Indeed, the prime test of an effective defense establishment in the contemporary world is that it be *potentially* powerful enough so it will *never* be used.

Because of the nature of the industry, investments in military production have a "low velocity" impact on the rest of the economy. (Or, in Keynsian terms, they have a low "multiplier" effect throughout the rest of the economy.) Much of the billions of dollars spent on defense each year is, in this sense, spent only once. It does not rebound through the economy to multiply other jobs and goods.

As an oversimplified illustration, the civilian automotive industries in Britain, Canada, the Federal Republic of Germany, France, Japan and the United States regularly generate thousands of dependent and derivative industries, services and jobs—auto accessories and repair services, service stations, superhighways, auto radios, roadside services, restaurants and motels, tourism and recreation, drive-in movies and supermarket centers. By contrast, the manufacture of military vehicles and tanks is, comparatively speaking, dead-end investment as far as the rest of the economy is concerned.

This suggests that conversion from an armed to a disarmed economy—provided investment and production levels were maintained, and effective consumption of goods and services were expanded proportionately—would accomplish two major benefits for the growth of the whole economy: (a) a net increase in the *quantity* of dollars available for productive enterprise and (b) greatly increased *velocity* for each of these dollars. In short, the whole economy would be capable of growing faster because each investment dollar could be more productive as it rebounded or multiplied throughout the disarmed economy.

ARMAMENTS AND ECONOMIC GROWTH

Some authorities argue that the relatively low growth rates and high unemployment rates in the U.S., British and Canadian economies in recent years are partly due to the relatively high proportion of national product that is devoted to defense purposes in these countries. The Federal Republic of Germany and Japan, by contrast, have had considerably lower defense budgets, in proportion to national product, plus far more rapid growth rates and insignificant unemployment rates.

The U.S. military budget for 1957-59 averaged 58.3 percent of gross domestic fixed capital formation and the U.S. unemployment rate ran at about 5.6 percent for the same period, while the Federal Republic of Germany's defense budget was averaging 16.7 per cent of gross domestic investment and unemployment was under 1 percent. Other factors were involved, of course, including proportionately heavier U.S. outlays of foreign economic and military aid and the steady flow— before the Berlin wall—of highly skilled East German refugee labor into the West German economy. Nonetheless, analysts have found some consistency in the relationship between defense spending on the one hand, and growth and unemployment rates on the other hand, in most of the industrialized nations (except for the centrally planned economies, which report no unemployment levels.)

In summary, the problems of converting a highly industrialized and heavily armed national economy to disarmament would probably be tempered and eased by the following factors:

1. Willingness and capacity of private and public interests in the society to plan, invest and work cooperatively toward minimum economic and social hardship and waste.

2. Speed of the adjustment process imposed by the disarmament agreement, and the resulting latitude for cushioning the impact of conversion.

3. The draft which the international peace and disarmament authorities might make on otherwise surplus manpower and other resources.

4. Economic dynamism and social creativeness which would probably be released simply by the conversion of defense capital to socially more productive capital.

ADJUSTMENT PROBLEMS OF DEVELOPING ECONOMIES

General and complete disarmament would not be an exclusively national problem for any country. In addition to the obvious international problems of disarmament inspection, supervision and enforcement, there would probably be major problems of trade dislocation. Comprehensive disarmament would certainly influence world demand (and prices) for strategic materials such as petroleum, natural rubber, tungsten, chrome, antimony, cobalt, tin, bauxite and other commodities which come primarily from the developing areas of the world.

Effective conversion to civilian production in the industrialized nations will no doubt take up some of the slack in world demand which disarmament would create. However, *any* drop in commodity export levels and prices will seriously aggravate the balance of payments problems of the developing nations. Many of these nations are already at the mercy of unstable world market prices for their commodity exports. At the same time, the prices for their essential imports, especially machinery and other capital goods, have steadily risen in the last decade. Furthermore, the capacity of most developing nations to pay for their own development out of trade earnings has generally lagged behind their aspirations and plans. Worse, this capacity has frequently been insufficient to keep pace with domestic population growth and with rates of world economic growth. In fact, the gap in living levels, between the industrialized nations and many of the developing nations, has actually increased rather than narrowed in recent years.

GLOBAL ECONOMIC PERSPECTIVES

With or without universal disarmament, most experts agree, economic relations between rich and poor nations call for major overhaul. This is, of course, an important function of contemporary foreign aid and a by-product of foreign private investment—to help the emerging nations reach the point where their economic growth will be self-sustaining.

With the advent of universal disarmament, the need for overhaul would become more urgent. The industrialized nations hold the key to peaceful conversion of the world economy—because of their superior productive capacity and resiliency, because they are capable of expanding mutually beneficial two-way trade with the developing economies, and because they have the capacity to export capital for both profitable purposes and for development assistance. In fact, a long-term effect of development assistance—foreign aid—should be to increase the purchasing power of the emerging economies and thus expand foreign markets for the industrialized nations.

UNFILLED NEEDS OF AN ARMED WORLD

There is a large backlog of jobs to be done throughout the world, in the industrialized as well as the developing societies. If a substantial part of the resources now devoted to defense purposes could be redirected to these needs, disarmament would indeed prove a boon to all mankind. The UN consultative study, "Economic and Social Consequences of Disarmament," which had the concurrence of both the United States and the Soviet Union, listed the following priority needs throughout the world economy:

"Raising standards of personal consumption of goods and services;

"Expanding or modernizing productive capacity through investment in new plant and equipment;

"Promoting housing construction, urban renewal, including slum clearance, and rural development;

"Improving and expanding facilities for education, health, welfare, social security, cultural development, scientific research, etc."

The magnitude of the job is illustrated by some of the national estimates cited in the study. In housing, for example, Latin America may require a $1.4 billion a year investment for thirty years to wipe out the current backlog. India estimates it will need $1 billion a year to house new inhabitants in its cities of over 100,000 population. U.S. urban renewal needs for 1960-65 were estimated at $20 billion a year for slum clearance, low income housing and community redevelopment, although only a part of that investment is actually being made.

In education, the United States estimates a 50 percent increase by 1970 in its annual outlay for elementary and secondary education (now running about $20 billion a year) and a 250 percent increase in costs of higher education (now running $6.7 billion a year). Western European outlays for education may rise from $9 billion a year in 1958 to $18 billion by 1970. Thirty-five nations and territories of tropical Africa would like to raise their annual investment in education to $1.1 billion by 1965, $1.8 billion in 1970 and $2.6 billion in 1980— provided sufficient foreign aid is forthcoming to bridge the gap between local resources and targeted expenditures.

In summary, the economics of disarmament are essentially the economics of great opportunities. The problem is not to find socially more productive uses for current defense outlays; it is to manage the transfer of these resources creatively and efficiently. This will require something more than economic analysis and managerial skill, however. The political climate, and the nature of international competition or cooperation in a disarmed world will have a bearing on the process.

POLITICS OF DISARMAMENT

The U.S. and Soviet draft disarmament treaties (and the Clark-Sohn treaty summary as well) do not presume that the major political problems which now divide the world would disappear with the adoption of universal disarmament. On the contrary, these disarmaments proposals take it for granted that the cold war confrontation would continue, along with rivalries among the lesser powers. The major political disputes of our time—Cuba, Berlin, Laos, Taiwan, Kashmir, South Africa, Angola, Arab-Israeli differences, and divided Germany, Korea and Vitnam—would also presumably remain with us.

General and complete disarmament would reduce or eliminate the danger of international violence in these disputes, but would not necessarily dispose of the underlying issues.

There is room for speculation, therefore, on what the political climate would be in a disarmed world. For example, would there be strong pressures to bring some of these disputes to a head and to try to resolve them? In the absence of national military power to force (or prevent) conflict resolution, what recourse would the disputing parties have? If a border dispute, or a delicate issue like Berlin, were to explode in violence at the small arms level, and the peace-keeping authority were authorized to intervene, how would the basic political conflict be disposed of? Or would governments in a disarmed world have to learn to live with the frustration of permanent, unresolvable political conflicts?

Even more important, what would be the political climate for the peoples of the world—as individuals and as members of different racial, national, religious and cultural groups? Would their personal security and their political rights be weakened or enhanced by disarmament? Would they feel less secure because their governments no longer had the power to defend them—or more secure because of the protection afforded by new international or world institutions? Would politically deprived minorities, or other groups with political or economic grievances, have to learn to live permanently with their frustrations?

All these questions are obviously related to the kinds of institutions and processes, political and juridical, which a disarmament plan would bring into being. Complete national disarmament would eliminate the ultimate governing factor in today's world political system. The political climate of a disarmed world—for national governments and for peoples —would depend on what institutions, if any, were created to fill this vacuum.

The Soviet disarmament proposal, as noted earlier, proposes no new machinery for resolving international conflicts. In fact, by demanding a return to a strict construction of the UN Charter, the Soviet plan would hardly impair the sovereignty of the five major powers. It would also insure against any international intervention in any dispute contrary to the interests of any of these major powers. For the governments of the smaller nations, international politics would be somewhat more restrictive than at present—their only appeal in an international dispute would be to the unanimity of the five permanent members of the UN Security Council.

The U.S. disarmament plan would create a different international political climate. No major power would be able to obstruct international intervention in a dispute. The final court of appeal for any nation, great or small, would presumably be the UN General Assembly. In a crisis situation, the Assembly could mobilize a powerful UN peace force to impose a solution to a dispute. In addition, the plan calls for expanded jurisdiction of the International Court over legal disputes and a strengthening of international law to guide conflict-resolution.

The Clark-Sohn plan goes much further. It proposes compulsory adjudication of legal disputes and enforced resolution of any dangerous political dispute. It is also much more specific in its peace-force proposals—the UN force would have a definite monopoly on military power. Finally, the Clark-Sohn plan calls for world legislative, executive and judicial institutions, including a system of regional UN courts authorized to try individual violators of the world disarmament law.

The three disarmament proposals represent a very wide political spectrum. The fundamental distinction between plans is where ultimate political authority would be lodged — with disarmed and sovereign national governments, supervised by a world directorate of the five major powers (Soviet plan); with a UN made up of sovereign and disarmed states but with considerable military power and some expanded jurisdiction (U.S. plan); or with a new world legislative, executive and judicial authority, commanding a world monopoly on military power.

Clearly the problem is one of relative risks in the political sphere. Put simply, the question is, How much political authority must be delegated to international or world agencies if disarmament is to be enforceable and the political climate is to be endurable?

Disarmament inescapably involves the sacrifice of a traditional prerogative of national sovereignty—the right to use or threaten to use force in support of national aims and interests. What other aspects of traditional national sovereignty must be delegated if disarmament is even to work? If the transfer of sovereignty must be substantial, then a very old problem arises in a new form: What safeguards would be necessary to insure that the world authority does not abuse its power?

DANGERS OF A WORLD POWER MONOPOLY

It is not unreasonable to assume that the process of creating a single world military monopoly might well be an irreversible process. Indeed, Clark and Sohn imply this when they propose a UN peace force "of such strength and armament as to be able *quickly* and *certainly* to prevent or suppress *any* international violence . . . any attack by nation against nation or any possible revolt against its own authority. . . ."

Eliminating the possibility of rebellion in the world eliminates the final recourse which people have used throughout history in resisting or overcoming tyranny. The Clark-Sohn plan attempts to deal with this danger by giving the people of the world an indirect voice in the management of world affairs—by creating a world legislature whose members would ultimately be elected by universal popular vote. This world legislature—either a greatly strengthened UN General Assembly or the General Conference of a World Disarmament and World Development Organization—would have only those powers delegated to it by the peoples and governments of the world. Essentially these would be the powers to enforce disarmament and maintain international peace. Yet there would also be certain essential related powers, including a taxing authority to insure adequate and reliable revenues.

Additional safeguards against tyranny would include a vast strengthening of international law, the creation of some measure of world law, and the establishment of a comprehensive world judicial and conciliation system. The authority of the peace force would be carefully defined and circumscribed and its command would be subject to civilian executive control and legislative review. The peace force would also be internationalized in the sense that participation would be limited to volunteers recruited on a quota which allowed no nation or group of nations to dominate the force.

Yet the basic conditions for the creation of an invulnerable global tyranny might still be present. It is conceivable that the world legislature might come under the domination of an elite willing to employ force for its own ends. Or the peace force—an absolute military power with its own *esprit de corps* and professional leadership—might rebel against the world authority. It would be the only power left in the world that would be capable of defying, not only national governments, but also the world executive and legislative bodies.

It is perhaps equally conceivable that the elimination of national armaments and the creation of viable political and judicial institutions on a global scale would lead to a profound transformation in the attitudes, tensions and fears of peoples and governments. If man can be released from the burden of armaments and the fear of war, he may also be released from the destructive psychology a war system fosters. The politics, as well as the economics, of a disarmed world may turn out to be infinitely more creative and constructive than past history has anticipated.

LOOKING AHEAD

In the final analysis, if the world is to disarm it must look for some balance between national power and international authority, between global security against war and the security of nations and peoples against tyranny. The ultimate value is man. A world system which protects man from war must also reflect his aspirations, his desire for change and his right to grant his consent or withhold it from those he places in positions of authority. Any new world system must be a satisfactory political system as well as a stable peace system.

SUGGESTED READINGS:

MENDLOVITZ, pp. 737-854.

ADDITIONAL READINGS:

BENOIT, EMILE. "Would Disarmament Mean a Depression?" *New York Times Magazine,* Apr. 28, 1963: 16.

BUSH, VANNEVAR. "Can Men Live Without War?" *Atlantic Monthly* 197: 35-38 (Feb. 1956).

PIEL, GERARD. "The Economics of Disarmament." *Bul. Atomic Scientists* 16: 117-122 (Apr. 1960).

SCHELLING, T. C. "Arms Control Will Not Cut Defense Costs." *Harvard Business Review* 39: 6-15 (Mar.–Apr. 1961).

REFERENCES:

BENOIT, EMILE and KENNETH E. BOULDING (editors). *Disarmament and the Economy.* NY: Harper and Row, 1963.

MELMAN, SEYMOUR (editor). *Disarmament: Its Politics and Economics.* Boston: American Academy of Arts and Sciences, 1962.

"Problems and Promises of a Warless World." A continuing series of articles in the *Saturday Review* by outstanding writers and thinkers including Arnold Toynbee, Walter Millis, Arthur Larson, and Margaret Mead, that consider various aspects of achieving and maintaining a world without war. See issues of May 12, Sept. 15, Oct. 6, Nov. 17, 1962; Feb. 16, June 1, June 22, 1963.

Session Nine   QUESTIONS FOR REFLECTION OR DISCUSSION

1. Is conversion from an armed to a disarmed economy a manageable task?

How would your job or profession, or the economy of your community, be affected by general and complete disarmament? What local industries would have to convert, cut back or close? Are defense industry and/or military payrolls vital to business in the community?

What current manpower and employment problems in the community would be aggravated or alleviated by disarmament. How?

Is there a backlog of unfilled needs in the community—education, worker training or retraining, housing, industrial plant modernization or expansion, rural development, health, welfare, cultural facilities, recreation, etc.?

Is there any interest in or attention to the problems of disarmament conversion in your community or state? Should there be? Why or why not?

What, in your opinion, are the most important problems your country would face in managing the conversion from an armed to a disarmed economy and society?

2. What problems and opportunities would universal disarmament create for world economic and social development?

In a disarming world, what principles should guide the industrialized nations in their relations with the developing societies? Should foreign aid be modified in any way—changed emphasis, some increase, substantial increase? Should aid continue to be primarily an instrument of national foreign policy? Or should all or most aid be channeled through an international authority?

What role should private investment play in world economic development?

What are the political implications, in a *disarmed* world, of (a) high levels of government-to-government foreign aid, (b) high levels of aid channeled through an international authority, and (c) high levels of private foreign investment?

3. What would be the political climate for the individual in a disarmed world?

What specific powers should the people of the world delegate to an international authority in order to insure that disarmament will be enforced and the peace will be stable?

What safeguards would be required to insure peoples and their governments against undue interference, by the world authority, in their private and domestic affairs? in their cultural and legal traditions?

In your opinion, how would an effective disarmament system, under law, affect the attitudes, fears and aspirations of peoples? Would it be likely to affect international politics as well? If so, in what possible ways?

SUMMARY QUESTION:

Recognizing that the basic cultural, ideological, political and other differences which divide the world today would also function in a disarmed world, what are the prospects for international cooperation under disarmament? Is "war-prevention" enough of a common global objective to bring some stability to the international system? How would the system operate if deep cold war hostilities continued under disarmament? Are there any other common global objectives—in addition to war-prevention—which could help hold the international system together?